# AFFILIATE MARKETING SECRETS GUIDE FOR BEGINNERS

Easy way to Generate Passive Income Online
and the simple strategy to follow

## Kane Schiller

# Copyright

© [2024] by All rights reserved.

No part of this publication may be reproduced, distributed, or transmitted in any form or by any means, including photocopying, recording, or other electronic or mechanical methods, without the prior written permission of the publisher, except in the case of brief quotations embodied in critical reviews and certain other noncommercial uses permitted by copyright law.

# Table of Contents

**Copyright**   1
**Table of Contents**   2
**Introduction**   4
**Introduction**   7
   Why Affiliate Marketing is a Great Opportunity 10
**Chapter 1: Understanding Affiliate Marketing**   17
   What is Affiliate Marketing?   22
   Key Players: Merchants, Affiliates, and Consumers   28
   How Affiliate Marketing Works   34
   Benefits of Affiliate Marketing   41
**Chapter 2: Choosing the Right Niche**   46
   Importance of Niche Selection   50
   Popular Affiliate Marketing Niches   55
   How to Identify a Profitable Niche   60
   Tools for Niche Research   64
**Chapter 3: Finding and Joining Affiliate Programs**   70
   Top Affiliate Networks to Join   75
   Evaluating Affiliate Programs   81
   How to Sign Up and Get Approved   86
   Understanding Commission Structures   90
**Chapter 4: Building Your Platform**   95
   Creating a Website or Blog   100
   Leveraging Social Media for Affiliate Marketing 105
   Email Marketing for Affiliates   110

|   |   |
|---|---|
| Content Creation Strategies | 116 |
| **Chapter 5: Traffic Generation Strategies** | **123** |
| SEO Basics for Affiliate Marketers | 128 |
| Paid Advertising Options | 134 |
| Utilizing Social Media for Traffic | 139 |
| Building an Engaged Audience | 144 |
| **Chapter 6: Secrets to Maximizing Your Earnings** | **150** |
| The Art of Persuasive Content | 156 |
| Building Trust with Your Audience | 160 |
| High-Conversion Techniques | 165 |
| Tracking and Analyzing Performance | 170 |
| **Appendix** | **176** |
| Glossary of Affiliate Marketing Terms | 179 |
| Recommended Tools and Resources | 185 |
| Sample Email Templates | 190 |
| Additional Reading and References | 195 |
| **Conclusion** | **200** |
| Recap of Key Points | 202 |
| Developing a Long-Term Strategy | 205 |
| Staying Updated with Industry Trends | 210 |
| Final Words of Encouragement | 213 |

# Introduction

There was a young man named Alex who was eager to find a way to supplement his income and achieve financial independence. Like many others, he turned to the internet in search of opportunities. After hours of browsing, Alex stumbled upon a book titled "Affiliate Marketing Secrets Guide for Beginners."

Intrigued by the promise of uncovering secrets to success in affiliate marketing, Alex wasted no time in purchasing the book. He delved into its pages with enthusiasm, absorbing every word and insight shared by the author. As he read, Alex felt a sense of clarity and excitement building within him. He realized that affiliate marketing could be the path he had been searching for.

Armed with newfound knowledge and determination, Alex set out to apply the strategies outlined in the book. He carefully selected a niche that aligned with his interests and began researching affiliate programs within that niche.

With the guidance from the book, Alex learned how to identify high-quality products and create compelling content to promote them.

As days turned into weeks, Alex dedicated himself to building his affiliate marketing business. He optimized his website for search engines, crafted engaging blog posts and product reviews, and leveraged social media to expand his reach. With each passing day, Alex's efforts began to bear fruit.

Then, one fateful morning, Alex received an email notification that changed everything. It was a commission notification from one of the affiliate programs he had joined. His heart raced as he opened the email to find that he had earned his first $500 in affiliate commissions. The excitement and sense of accomplishment that washed over him were indescribable.

Buoyed by his initial success, Alex doubled down on his efforts. He continued to refine his strategies, experiment with new tactics, and scale up his affiliate marketing campaigns. Before long, his earnings surpassed the $1,000 mark, and then kept climbing higher and higher.

As Alex reflected on his journey, he couldn't help but marvel at how far he had come. From reading a book titled "Affiliate Marketing Secrets Guide for Beginners" to achieving his first $500 to $1,000 in affiliate commissions, it had been an incredible ride. With perseverance, dedication, and the right knowledge, Alex had turned his dreams of financial freedom into reality through the power of affiliate marketing. And this was just the beginning of his journey to even greater heights of success.

# Introduction

Welcome to the world of affiliate marketing! If you've been searching for a reliable way to generate passive income online, you've come to the right place. This guide is designed specifically for beginners, providing you with the secrets and strategies to kickstart your journey in affiliate marketing and turn it into a profitable venture.

**What is Affiliate Marketing?**

Affiliate marketing is a performance-based marketing strategy where you, the affiliate, earn a commission for promoting someone else's products or services. It's a win-win situation: businesses expand their reach and sales, while you earn income by recommending products you believe in. The beauty of affiliate marketing lies in its simplicity and potential for passive income. Once you set up your system, it can continue to generate revenue with minimal ongoing effort.

**Benefits of Affiliate Marketing for Beginners**

Affiliate marketing offers several advantages, especially for those just starting out:

- **Low Startup Costs:** You don't need to create your own products or maintain inventory. Your primary investment is your time and effort.
- **Flexibility and Freedom:** You can work from anywhere and choose products that align with your interests and expertise.
- **Scalability:** As you gain experience, you can expand your efforts, promote more products, and increase your earnings.
- **Passive Income Potential:** Once established, your affiliate marketing efforts can generate income around the clock, even while you sleep.

**Overview of the Guide**

This guide will walk you through the entire process of becoming a successful affiliate marketer. Whether you're looking to make a little extra money on the side or replace your full-time income, the strategies and insights shared here will set you on the right path.

**Here's a brief overview of what you'll learn:**

- **Chapter 1: Understanding Affiliate Marketing** – Dive into the fundamentals of affiliate marketing, learn how it works, and discover how to choose a profitable niche.

- **Chapter 2: Finding Profitable Affiliate Programs** – Learn how to identify high-converting products and evaluate affiliate programs to maximize your earnings.

- **Chapter 3: Building Your Affiliate Platform** – Find out how to create a compelling online presence through websites, blogs, and social media.

- **Chapter 4: Driving Traffic to Your Affiliate Links** – Explore effective strategies for attracting and engaging your target audience.

- **Chapter 5: Conversion Optimization Secrets** – Uncover the secrets to turning your traffic into sales through optimized content and marketing techniques.

- **Chapter 6: Scaling Your Affiliate Marketing Business** – Learn how to automate and scale your business for long-term growth and increased profitability.

In addition to these chapters, you'll also find sections dedicated to the secrets of successful affiliate marketers, advanced strategies, and an appendix filled with valuable resources.

By the end of this guide, you'll have a comprehensive understanding of affiliate marketing and the tools needed to succeed. Let's Kickstart on this exciting journey together and see the secrets to generating passive income online through affiliate marketing!

# Why Affiliate Marketing is a Great Opportunity

Affiliate marketing has emerged as one of the most attractive online business models, offering numerous benefits that make it an excellent opportunity for beginners and seasoned entrepreneurs alike.

**These are some compelling reasons why affiliate marketing is a great opportunity:**

**1. Low Startup Costs**

One of the most significant advantages of affiliate marketing is its low barrier to entry. Unlike traditional businesses that require substantial capital for inventory, staff, and physical storefronts, affiliate marketing requires minimal investment. All you need is a computer, internet connection, and some time to create content. This makes it an accessible option for anyone looking to start a business with limited resources.

**2. No Need for Product Creation**

Creating your own products can be time-consuming, expensive, and risky. With affiliate marketing, you don't need to worry about product development, manufacturing, or logistics. You simply promote existing products and earn commissions on sales. This allows you to focus on marketing and building your audience without the complexities of managing a product-based business.

## 3. Flexibility and Independence

Affiliate marketing offers unparalleled flexibility. You can work from anywhere in the world, set your own hours, and create a business that fits your lifestyle. This independence makes affiliate marketing an attractive option for those seeking to escape the confines of a traditional 9-to-5 job. Whether you want to work part-time or full-time, affiliate marketing can adapt to your schedule.

## 4. Passive Income Potential

One of the most appealing aspects of affiliate marketing is the potential for passive income. Once you've set up your affiliate links and created content, your efforts can continue to generate revenue long after the initial work is done. This means you can earn money while you sleep, travel, or spend time with your family. Over time, as you build more content and optimize your strategies, your passive income can grow significantly.

**5. Scalability**

Affiliate marketing is highly scalable. As you gain experience and develop effective marketing strategies, you can expand your efforts to promote more products, enter new niches, and increase your earnings. There are no limits to how much you can grow your affiliate marketing business. With the right approach, you can scale your income exponentially.

**6. Diverse Income Streams**

Affiliate marketing allows you to diversify your income streams by promoting a wide range of products and services across different niches. This diversification reduces your risk and increases your earning potential. By partnering with multiple affiliate programs, you can create a robust portfolio of income sources, ensuring that your business remains resilient even if one product or niche underperforms.

**7. Performance-Based Rewards**

In affiliate marketing, your earnings are directly tied to your performance. The more effective you are at driving traffic and conversions, the more money you make. This performance-based model rewards creativity, effort, and strategic thinking. It also means there's no cap on your income potential – the sky's the limit if you're willing to put in the work.

**8. Continuous Learning and Growth**

The world of affiliate marketing is dynamic and ever-evolving. Staying updated with the latest trends, tools, and strategies is essential for success. This constant need for learning and adaptation makes affiliate marketing an intellectually stimulating and fulfilling career. You'll have the opportunity to develop new skills, explore various marketing techniques, and continually improve your business.

**9. Access to a Global Market**

Affiliate marketing enables you to reach a global audience. The internet has no geographical boundaries, meaning you can promote products to people all over the world. This vast potential market increases your chances of finding a receptive audience and achieving higher sales volumes.

**10. Supportive Community and Resources**

The affiliate marketing community is vast and supportive, offering a wealth of resources, forums, and networks where you can learn, share experiences, and seek advice. Numerous blogs, podcasts, webinars, and courses are available to help you enhance your skills and stay informed about industry trends.

Affiliate marketing presents a fantastic opportunity for anyone looking to generate passive income online. Its low startup costs, flexibility, scalability, and potential for passive income make it an ideal business model for beginners and experienced marketers alike. By leveraging the power of affiliate marketing, you can create a profitable and sustainable online business that fits your lifestyle and financial goals.

# Chapter 1: Understanding Affiliate Marketing

Affiliate marketing is a powerful and accessible way to earn money online by promoting products or services offered by other companies. In this chapter, we'll explore the fundamentals of affiliate marketing, how it works, and how you can choose a profitable niche that aligns with your interests and expertise.

**The Basics of Affiliate Marketing**

At its core, affiliate marketing is a performance-based marketing strategy where a business rewards an affiliate for each visitor or customer brought by the affiliate's marketing efforts.

**How the process typically works:**

**1. Join an Affiliate Program:** You sign up for an affiliate program offered by a company or affiliate network. This program provides you with unique affiliate links to promote their products or services.

**2. Promote Products:** You incorporate these affiliate links into your content, which could be blog posts, social media posts, emails, or other marketing channels.

**3. Drive Traffic:** Your goal is to drive traffic to these links by attracting and engaging your audience.

**4. Earn Commissions:** When someone clicks on your affiliate link and makes a purchase, you earn a commission. The commission rate varies depending on the affiliate program and product category.

**How Affiliate Marketing Works**

To understand how affiliate marketing works, let's break down the key components involved in the process:

- **Merchant (Advertiser):** The company that creates and sells the product or service. They provide the affiliate program and pay commissions to affiliates.

- **Affiliate (Publisher):** You, the marketer who promotes the merchant's products through unique affiliate links.

- **Consumer:** The end user who clicks on the affiliate link and makes a purchase.

- **Affiliate Network:** An intermediary platform that connects affiliates with merchants. Examples include Commission Junction (CJ), ShareASale, and ClickBank. Networks provide tracking, reporting, and payment solutions.

## Key Terms and Concepts

- **Affiliate Link:** A unique URL assigned to an affiliate that tracks traffic and sales generated from their marketing efforts.

- **Commission:** The amount of money paid to an affiliate for each sale, lead, or action generated through their affiliate link.

- **Conversion Rate:** The percentage of visitors who complete a desired action (e.g., making a purchase) after clicking on an affiliate link.

- **Cookie Duration:** The length of time a cookie (a small piece of data stored on the user's device) tracks the user's activity. This duration affects whether an affiliate receives credit for a sale if the user returns later to make a purchase.

**Choosing Your Niche**

Selecting the right niche is a critical step in your affiliate marketing journey. Your niche is the specific segment of the market you will target with your marketing efforts.

**The tips to help you choose a profitable niche:**

**1. Identify Your Interests and Expertise:** Start by listing topics you are passionate about or have knowledge in. Your enthusiasm and expertise will make it easier to create engaging content and connect with your audience.

**2. Research Market Demand:** Use tools like Google Trends, Keyword Planner, and social media insights to gauge the popularity and demand for your potential niches. Look for niches with a high search volume and consistent interest over time.

**3. Analyze Competition:** Evaluate the level of competition in your chosen niches. High competition can indicate a profitable market, but it also means you'll need to find ways to differentiate yourself. Low competition might be easier to break into, but ensure there is enough demand to sustain your efforts.

**4. Evaluate Affiliate Programs:** Check if there are reputable affiliate programs available in your niche. Look for programs that offer attractive commissions, quality products, and good support for affiliates.

**5. Assess Monetization Potential:** Consider the types of products or services you can promote in your niche. Higher-priced items or those with recurring commissions (such as subscriptions) can significantly increase your earning potential.

Understanding the basics of affiliate marketing is the first step towards building a successful affiliate marketing business. By grasping how it works and choosing the right niche, you lay a solid foundation for your future efforts. In the next chapter, we'll delve deeper into finding profitable affiliate programs that align with your niche and goals. Let's move forward and continue building your path to passive income through affiliate marketing.

## What is Affiliate Marketing?

Affiliate marketing is a performance-based online marketing strategy where businesses reward affiliates (marketers) for driving traffic, leads, or sales to their products or services. This model leverages the marketing efforts of affiliates to reach a broader audience, while affiliates earn commissions based on their performance. It's a mutually beneficial arrangement that has become a cornerstone of e-commerce and digital marketing.

**How Affiliate Marketing Works**

**At its core, affiliate marketing involves three main parties:**

**1. Merchant (Advertiser):** The company or individual that creates and sells a product or service. Merchants can range from large retailers like Amazon to small businesses and even solo entrepreneurs.

**2. Affiliate (Publisher):** The marketer who promotes the merchant's products or services. Affiliates can be bloggers, influencers, website owners, or anyone with an online presence who can reach potential customers.

**3. Consumer:** The end user who sees the affiliate's marketing efforts, clicks on an affiliate link, and makes a purchase or completes another desired action (such as signing up for a newsletter).

**The Affiliate Marketing Process**

**The step-by-step breakdown of how the affiliate marketing process typically works:**

**1. Join an Affiliate Program:** The affiliate signs up for an affiliate program provided by a merchant or through an affiliate network. Upon approval, the affiliate receives a unique affiliate link or code to track their referrals.

**2. Promote Products or Services:** The affiliate incorporates the affiliate link into their content. This can be through blog posts, social media posts, videos, emails, or other marketing channels.

**3. Drive Traffic:** The affiliate aims to attract and engage an audience that is interested in the promoted products or services. Effective strategies include content marketing, search engine optimization (SEO), paid advertising, and social media marketing.

**4. Track and Analyze:** When consumers click on the affiliate link, they are directed to the merchant's website, and their actions are tracked using cookies or other tracking mechanisms. The affiliate can monitor their performance using dashboards provided by the affiliate program or network.

**5. Earn Commissions:** If the consumer completes a desired action (such as making a purchase or filling out a form), the affiliate earns a commission. The commission structure varies by program and can be a percentage of the sale, a fixed amount per conversion, or other forms of compensation.

**Key Components and Terms**

- **Affiliate Link:** A unique URL or code that tracks the traffic and sales generated by an affiliate. This link ensures that the affiliate receives credit for their marketing efforts.
- **Commission:** The payment an affiliate receives for driving a successful action, such as a sale or lead. Commission rates vary widely depending on the product, niche, and affiliate program.
- **Cookie Duration:** The length of time a cookie (a small piece of data stored in the user's browser) tracks the user's activity after clicking on an affiliate link. This determines the timeframe in which the affiliate can earn a commission if the user makes a purchase.
- **Conversion Rate:** The percentage of visitors who take the desired action after clicking on an affiliate link. A higher conversion rate indicates more effective marketing efforts.

**Benefits of Affiliate Marketing**

- **Low Startup Costs:** Unlike traditional businesses, affiliate marketing requires minimal initial investment. You don't need to create products or maintain inventory.

- **Passive Income Potential:** Once set up, affiliate marketing can generate ongoing income with relatively little maintenance. High-quality content can continue to attract visitors and earn commissions over time.

- **Flexibility:** You can work from anywhere with an internet connection and choose products and niches that align with your interests.

- **Scalability:** Successful affiliate marketing can be scaled by promoting more products, entering new niches, or employing advanced marketing techniques.

**Challenges of Affiliate Marketing**

**While affiliate marketing offers many advantages, it also comes with challenges:**

- **High Competition:** Popular niches can be highly competitive, making it difficult to stand out.

- **Income Variability:** Affiliate earnings can be unpredictable, especially in the early stages.
- **Dependence on Merchant Policies:** Affiliates rely on merchants to provide reliable tracking, timely payments, and quality products. Changes in merchant policies can impact your earnings.

Affiliate marketing is a compelling way to generate income online by promoting products and services you believe in. By understanding the basics and key components, you can begin to navigate this lucrative field and start building a profitable affiliate marketing business. In the following chapters, we will explore how to find profitable affiliate programs, build an effective affiliate platform, and implement strategies to drive traffic and optimize conversions.

# Key Players: Merchants, Affiliates, and Consumers

Affiliate marketing is a symbiotic ecosystem involving three main players: merchants, affiliates, and consumers. Each of these roles is crucial to the success of the affiliate marketing model. Let's explore the responsibilities and significance of each key player.

**1. Merchants (Advertisers)**

**Who are Merchants?**

Merchants, also known as advertisers, are businesses or individuals who create and sell products or services. They initiate affiliate programs to extend their marketing reach and increase sales by leveraging the promotional efforts of affiliates.

**Roles and Responsibilities:**

- **Create Affiliate Programs:** Merchants design and manage affiliate programs, which include setting commission structures, providing marketing materials, and establishing terms and conditions.
- **Provide Products or Services:** Merchants ensure that their products or services are of high quality and meet customer expectations. They

handle inventory, order fulfillment, and customer service.

- **Track Performance:** Merchants use tracking software to monitor the performance of their affiliates, including clicks, conversions, and sales generated through affiliate links.

- **Pay Commissions:** Merchants are responsible for paying affiliates their earned commissions, typically on a monthly basis or according to the terms outlined in the affiliate program.

**Benefits for Merchants:**

- **Increased Reach:** Affiliates help merchants reach a broader audience, including potential customers they might not have accessed otherwise.

- **Performance-Based Marketing:** Merchants only pay for actual results, such as sales or leads, making affiliate marketing a cost-effective strategy.

- **Brand Awareness:** Affiliates promote the merchant's brand, products, or services, increasing overall brand awareness and credibility.

**2. Affiliates (Publishers)**

## Who are Affiliates?

Affiliates, also known as publishers, are individuals or entities that promote merchants' products or services to their audience. They can be bloggers, social media influencers, website owners, or even email marketers. Affiliates earn commissions based on the sales or leads they generate for the merchants.

### Roles and Responsibilities:

- **Promote Products or Services:** Affiliates create content that promotes the merchant's products or services. This can include blog posts, reviews, social media posts, videos, and email newsletters.
- **Drive Traffic:** Affiliates use various marketing strategies, such as SEO, paid advertising, and social media marketing, to drive traffic to the merchant's site through their affiliate links.
- **Engage Audience:** Affiliates build and engage their audience by providing valuable and relevant content that encourages clicks and conversions.

- **Track Performance:** Affiliates monitor their own performance using analytics tools to understand what strategies are working and to optimize their efforts for better results.

**Benefits for Affiliates:**

- **Income Potential:** Affiliates can earn a significant income through commissions, especially if they promote high-converting products or have a large, engaged audience.
- **Flexibility:** Affiliates can work from anywhere and have the freedom to choose which products or services to promote.
- **Low Risk:** Affiliates do not need to handle product creation, inventory management, or customer service, reducing their business risks.

## 3. Consumers

**Who are Consumers?**

Consumers are the end users who purchase products or services through the affiliate's promotional efforts. They are the ultimate target of affiliate marketing activities.

**Roles and Responsibilities:**

**- Engage with Content:** Consumers engage with the content created by affiliates, such as reading blog posts, watching videos, or following social media posts.

**- Click on Affiliate Links:** Consumers click on affiliate links embedded in the content, which directs them to the merchant's website.

**- Make Purchases or Take Actions:** Consumers make purchases or complete desired actions (like signing up for a newsletter) on the merchant's site, leading to commissions for affiliates.

**Benefits for Consumers:**

**- Informed Decisions:** Consumers benefit from the reviews, comparisons, and recommendations provided by affiliates, which help them make informed purchasing decisions.

- **Access to Deals:** Affiliates often share exclusive deals, discounts, or special offers with their audience, providing added value to consumers.

- **Quality Content:** Consumers receive high-quality, relevant content tailored to their interests and needs, enhancing their overall online experience.

Understanding the roles and responsibilities of the key players in affiliate marketing—merchants, affiliates, and consumers—is essential for navigating and succeeding in this field. Merchants provide the products and manage the affiliate programs, affiliates promote these products and drive traffic, and consumers engage with the content and make purchases. This collaborative ecosystem creates a win-win situation for all parties involved, fostering growth and success in the digital marketplace. In the next sections, we will delve deeper into how to find profitable affiliate programs and effectively promote products to maximize your affiliate marketing potential.

# How Affiliate Marketing Works

Affiliate marketing is a dynamic and effective business model that connects merchants with affiliates to promote products or services, creating a win-win situation for both parties.

**The detailed look at how affiliate marketing works:**

**1. The Players Involved**

**Merchants (Advertisers)**
- These are businesses or individuals who sell products or services.
- They create and manage affiliate programs to extend their reach and increase sales.
- **Examples:** Amazon, eBay, digital product creators, and service providers.

**Affiliates (Publishers)**
- These are individuals or entities who promote the merchant's products or services.

- They use various marketing strategies to attract an audience and drive traffic to the merchant's website.
- **Examples:** Bloggers, social media influencers, website owners, and email marketers.

### Consumers
- These are the end users who purchase products or services through the affiliate's marketing efforts.
- Their interactions with affiliate links drive the affiliate marketing process.

## 2. The Affiliate Marketing Process

### Step 1: Joining an Affiliate Program
- **Merchants** create affiliate programs, either in-house or through affiliate networks.
- **Affiliates** sign up for these programs. Upon approval, they receive unique affiliate links to promote the merchant's products.

### Step 2: Promoting Products or Services
- **Affiliates** integrate affiliate links into their content.

**This content can take various forms:**
- Blog posts
- Product reviews
- Social media posts
- YouTube videos
- Email newsletters
- Paid advertisements

**Step 3: Driving Traffic**
- **Affiliates** employ strategies to attract and engage their target audience.

**These strategies include:**
- Search Engine Optimization (SEO)
- Content marketing
- Social media marketing
- Paid advertising (e.g., Google Ads, Facebook Ads)
- Email marketing campaigns

**Step 4: Tracking and Analyzing Performance**
- **Merchants** and **affiliates** use tracking software and tools provided by the affiliate program to

monitor clicks, conversions, and sales generated through affiliate links.

- **Cookies** play a crucial role by storing data on the consumer's browser. This data ensures that affiliates receive credit for sales even if the purchase is made days or weeks later, depending on the cookie duration.

## Step 5: Earning Commissions

- **Consumers** make purchases or complete desired actions (e.g., filling out a form) on the merchant's website.

- **Affiliates** earn a commission for each conversion. The commission structure can vary:

    - **Pay-Per-Sale (PPS):** Affiliates earn a percentage of the sale price.
    - **Pay-Per-Click (PPC):** Affiliates earn a fee for each click generated.
    - **Pay-Per-Lead (PPL):** Affiliates earn a fee for each lead generated (e.g., sign-ups, form submissions).

## Step 6: Receiving Payments

- **Merchants** process and validate the sales or leads generated by affiliates.

- **Affiliates** receive their commissions according to the payment schedule defined by the affiliate program. Payments are usually made monthly via bank transfer, PayPal, or other payment methods.

**Key Terms and Concepts**

- **AffiliateLink:** A unique URL provided to affiliates to track their referrals and sales.

- **Commission:** The payment affiliates receive for driving a sale, lead, or click.

- **Cookie Duration:** The time period during which a cookie tracks a consumer's activity, ensuring that the affiliate gets credit for the sale if the consumer makes a purchase within this timeframe.

- **Conversion Rate:** The percentage of visitors who complete a desired action (e.g., making a purchase) after clicking on an affiliate link.

**Benefits of Affiliate Marketing**

**For Merchants:**

- **Cost-Effective Marketing:** Pay only for actual performance (sales or leads), reducing the risk of ineffective spending.

- **Extended Reach:** Leverage the affiliate's audience to reach potential customers.

- **Increased Sales:** Drive more sales through the efforts of multiple affiliates.

**For Affiliates:**

- **Income Potential:** Earn commissions by promoting products without the need to handle inventory or customer service.

- **Flexibility:** Work from anywhere and choose which products to promote.

- **Passive Income:** Once content is created and links are placed, affiliates can earn money passively as consumers make purchases over time.

**For Consumers:**

- **Informed Decisions:** Access valuable content, reviews, and recommendations from affiliates.

- **Exclusive Deals:** Affiliates often share special offers and discounts with their audience.

- **Convenience:** Easily find products and services tailored to their needs and interests.

Affiliate marketing is an efficient and effective way for merchants to boost their sales and for affiliates to earn income by promoting products they believe in. By understanding the roles of merchants, affiliates, and consumers, and the process that connects them, you can leverage this model to build a successful affiliate marketing business. In the next chapters, we will explore how to choose the right niche, find profitable affiliate programs, and employ strategies to maximize your earnings.

## Benefits of Affiliate Marketing

Affiliate marketing offers numerous benefits for both merchants and affiliates, making it a highly attractive business model in the digital landscape.

**Let's explore the key advantages of affiliate marketing:**

**Benefits for Merchants:**

**1. Cost-Effective Marketing:** Merchants only pay for actual results, such as sales or leads, rather than upfront advertising costs. This performance-based model minimizes the risk of ineffective marketing spending.

**2. Expanded Reach:** By leveraging the promotional efforts of affiliates, merchants can extend their reach to a broader audience. Affiliates often have niche-specific or highly engaged audiences that may be difficult for merchants to access through traditional marketing channels.

**3. Increased Sales:** Affiliate marketing can drive incremental sales for merchants by tapping into the trust and credibility established by affiliates with their audience. Affiliates' recommendations and endorsements can influence purchasing decisions, resulting in higher conversion rates.

**4. Diverse Marketing Channels:** Affiliate marketing allows merchants to diversify their marketing channels beyond traditional advertising.

Affiliates utilize various platforms and strategies, including blogs, social media, email marketing, and paid advertising, to promote products and services.

**5. Performance Tracking:** Merchants have access to robust tracking and analytics tools provided by affiliate networks or platforms. They can monitor key performance metrics, track affiliate activity, and optimize their marketing strategies based on real-time data insights.

**Benefits for Affiliates:**

**1. Income Potential:** Affiliates have the opportunity to earn passive income by promoting products or services and earning commissions on successful sales or leads. Depending on the niche, audience size, and marketing efforts, affiliates can generate significant revenue streams.

**2. Flexibility and Independence:** Affiliate marketing offers flexibility in terms of work schedule, location, and niche selection. Affiliates can work from anywhere with an internet connection and have the freedom to choose which products or services to promote, allowing for a customizable and scalable business model.

**3. Low Startup Costs:** Unlike traditional businesses that require significant upfront investment in inventory, infrastructure, and marketing, affiliate marketing has low barriers to entry. Affiliates can start with minimal investment in a website, domain, or promotional tools.

**4. No Product Creation or Inventory Management:** Affiliates do not need to create their own products or manage inventory, shipping, or customer service. This eliminates the complexities and overhead associated with product development and fulfillment, allowing affiliates to focus on marketing and promotion.

**5. Opportunity for Passive Income:** Once established, affiliate marketing can generate passive income streams as affiliates' content continues to attract traffic and drive conversions over time. High-quality evergreen content and strategic optimization can lead to ongoing revenue without constant active promotion.

**6. Diverse Income Streams:** Affiliates can diversify their income streams by promoting a wide range of products or services across different niches. This diversification helps mitigate risk and provides stability in fluctuating market conditions.

**7. Access to Training and Support:** Many affiliate programs and networks offer training resources, marketing materials, and dedicated support to help affiliates succeed. Affiliates can leverage these resources to enhance their skills, optimize their campaigns, and stay updated with industry trends.

Affiliate marketing presents a multitude of benefits for both merchants and affiliates, ranging from cost-effective marketing and expanded reach to income potential and flexibility. By understanding and leveraging these advantages, businesses and individuals can harness the power of affiliate marketing to drive sales, generate revenue, and build successful online ventures.

# Chapter 2: Choosing the Right Niche

Selecting the right niche is a crucial step in building a successful affiliate marketing business. A niche is a specific segment of the market that targets a particular audience with distinct needs, interests, and preferences. By choosing a niche that aligns with your expertise, interests, and audience's needs, you can maximize your chances of success in affiliate marketing.

**Guide to help you choose the right niche:**

**1. Identify Your Interests and Expertise:**

Start by brainstorming topics that you are passionate about or have knowledge and expertise in. Consider your hobbies, interests, skills, and professional experience. Your enthusiasm and expertise in a particular niche will not only make the process more enjoyable but also help you create valuable and engaging content for your audience.

**2. Research Market Demand:**

Use online tools such as Google Trends, Keyword Planner, and niche research websites to analyze the demand and popularity of potential niches. Look for niches with a consistent level of interest over time and a growing trend. Pay attention to search volume, keyword competition, and seasonal trends to identify evergreen niches with long-term potential.

**3. Evaluate Competition:**

Assess the level of competition in your chosen niches to determine your ability to stand out and succeed. While high competition may indicate a profitable market, it can also make it challenging to gain visibility and compete with established players. Consider niches with a balance of demand and competition, where you can differentiate yourself and add value to your audience.

**4. Consider Profitability:**

Evaluate the monetization potential of your chosen niche by researching affiliate programs, products, and commission rates available in the market. Look for niches with a diverse range of affiliate products or services, high-ticket items, recurring commissions, or affiliate programs with generous commission structures. Ensure that there is sufficient demand and purchasing power within your niche to generate sustainable income.

**5. Assess Audience Needs:**

Understand the needs, pain points, and preferences of your target audience within your chosen niche. Conduct market research, surveys, and audience analysis to identify common problems, questions, and interests that you can address through your content and affiliate promotions. Tailor your marketing efforts to provide solutions and value to your audience, building trust and credibility over time.

**6. Passion vs. Profitability:**

Strike a balance between your passion and profitability when choosing a niche. While it's essential to choose a niche that interests you and aligns with your passion, don't overlook the importance of profitability and market demand. Consider niches where your passion intersects with profitable opportunities, allowing you to leverage your expertise and enthusiasm to drive success.

**7. Long-Term Viability:**

Evaluate the long-term viability and sustainability of your chosen niche by considering industry trends, technological advancements, and evolving consumer preferences. Choose niches that are not only profitable and popular in the short term but also have the potential for long-term growth and relevance. Adaptability and flexibility are key to staying ahead in a dynamic and competitive market.

**8. Test and Validate:**

Finally, test and validate your chosen niche before fully committing to it. Start by creating content, promoting affiliate products, and engaging with your audience to gauge their response and feedback. Monitor key metrics such as traffic, engagement, conversion rates, and revenue to assess the viability and profitability of your niche. Iterate and refine your strategies based on data-driven insights to optimize your affiliate marketing efforts over time.

Choosing the right niche is a critical foundation for affiliate marketing success. By identifying a niche that aligns with your interests, expertise, audience needs, and profitability, you can create a sustainable and lucrative affiliate marketing business. Take the time to research, evaluate, and test different niches to find the perfect fit for your goals and aspirations. Remember that niche selection is not set in stone, and you can always pivot or expand into new niches as you grow and evolve in your affiliate marketing journey.

## Importance of Niche Selection

Niche selection is one of the most critical decisions you'll make in your affiliate marketing journey. Your niche determines who your target audience is, the type of content you create, the products you promote, and ultimately, your potential for success.

**The several reasons why niche selection is crucial in affiliate marketing:**

**1. Audience Relevance and Engagement:**

Choosing the right niche allows you to target a specific audience with common interests, needs, and preferences. By catering to a niche audience, you can create content that resonates deeply with them, leading to higher engagement, interaction, and trust. When your audience feels understood and valued, they are more likely to engage with your content and follow your recommendations.

**2. Differentiation and Competitive Advantage:**

Selecting a niche that is not oversaturated allows you to differentiate yourself from competitors and carve out a unique position in the market. By focusing on a niche with less competition or untapped opportunities, you can stand out as an authority or expert in your niche. Differentiation gives you a competitive advantage and increases your visibility, credibility, and influence within your niche.

**3. Monetization Potential and Profitability:**

Certain niches have higher monetization potential and profitability than others. By choosing a profitable niche with high demand, purchasing power, and affiliate opportunities, you can maximize your earning potential. Niches with specialized or high-ticket products, recurring commissions, or evergreen appeal offer greater opportunities for generating passive income and long-term revenue streams.

**4. Passion and Motivation:**

Selecting a niche that aligns with your interests, expertise, and passions can significantly impact your motivation and enjoyment in affiliate marketing. When you are passionate about your niche, you are more likely to invest time, effort, and creativity into creating valuable content and engaging with your audience. Passion fuels your enthusiasm, authenticity, and commitment, leading to sustained success and fulfillment in your affiliate marketing journey.

**5. Targeted Marketing and Conversion Rates:**

Niche marketing allows you to tailor your marketing efforts to the specific needs, preferences, and pain points of your target audience. By understanding your audience's motivations and challenges, you can create targeted content and promotions that resonate with them on a deeper level. Targeted marketing leads to higher conversion rates as you deliver relevant solutions and recommendations that address your audience's specific needs and desires.

**6. Scalability and Growth Opportunities:**

Choosing a niche with scalability and growth potential enables you to expand and diversify your affiliate marketing business over time. As you establish yourself in your niche and build a loyal audience, you can explore new sub-niches, products, or markets to further expand your reach and revenue streams. Scalability allows you to adapt to changing market trends, consumer preferences, and business opportunities, ensuring long-term viability and success.

**7. Risk Mitigation and Longevity:**

Niche selection plays a crucial role in mitigating risks and ensuring the longevity of your affiliate marketing business. By avoiding overly broad or volatile niches, you reduce the risk of market saturation, competition, and fluctuations. Choosing a niche with evergreen appeal, consistent demand, and enduring relevance provides a stable foundation for your business and minimizes the risk of obsolescence or downturns.

Niche selection is a fundamental aspect of affiliate marketing that influences every aspect of your business, from audience engagement and differentiation to monetization and scalability. By carefully choosing a niche that aligns with your interests, expertise, audience needs, and profitability, you can create a sustainable and successful affiliate marketing business. Take the time to research, evaluate, and validate different niches to find the perfect fit for your goals and aspirations. The niche selection is not a one-time decision but an ongoing process that evolves as you grow and adapt in your affiliate marketing journey.

# Popular Affiliate Marketing Niches

Affiliate marketing encompasses a vast array of niches, each with its own audience, products, and opportunities for monetization. While the profitability of niches may fluctuate over time, several niches have consistently remained popular and lucrative in the affiliate marketing industry.

**Some of the most popular affiliate marketing niches:**

**1. Health and Wellness:**
  - **Fitness Programs and Equipment:** From workout routines and fitness apps to gym equipment and apparel, the health and fitness niche offers a wide range of products for affiliate promotion.
  - **Nutritional Supplements:** Vitamins, protein powders, and dietary supplements are popular

products in the health and wellness niche, catering to consumers seeking improved health and fitness.

- **Weight Loss and Diet Plans:** Weight loss programs, meal replacement shakes, and diet plans are in high demand as people strive to achieve their weight loss goals.

2. **Personal Finance:**

- **Credit Cards and Banking:** Affiliate marketers can promote credit card offers, banking services, and financial products that help consumers manage their finances and save money.

- **Investing and Trading:** Investment platforms, brokerage services, and trading courses are sought after by individuals looking to grow their wealth and improve their financial literacy.

- **Budgeting and Saving:** Budgeting apps, savings accounts, and financial planning tools assist consumers in managing their expenses and achieving financial goals.

3. **Technology and Gadgets:**

- **Consumer Electronics:** Smartphones, laptops, tablets, and other gadgets are perennially popular products in the technology niche, appealing to tech-savvy consumers.

- **Software and Apps:** Productivity tools, mobile apps, and software solutions cater to individuals and businesses seeking to streamline their operations and enhance efficiency.

- **Gaming and Entertainment:** Video games, gaming consoles, streaming services, and entertainment subscriptions are highly sought after by gamers and entertainment enthusiasts.

**4. Lifestyle and Fashion:**

- **Beauty and Skincare:** Cosmetics, skincare products, and beauty treatments cater to consumers looking to enhance their appearance and self-care routines.

- **Fashion and Apparel:** Clothing, accessories, and footwear are perennially popular in the fashion niche, offering endless opportunities for affiliate promotion.

- **Home Decor and Interior Design:** Home decor items, furniture, and design services appeal to individuals looking to beautify their living spaces and express their personal style.

**5. Home and Garden:**

- **DIY and Home Improvement:** Tools, hardware, and DIY guides cater to homeowners and DIY enthusiasts seeking to renovate or improve their homes.

- **Gardening and Outdoor Living:** Gardening tools, plants, and outdoor furniture are popular products for individuals with green thumbs and outdoor living spaces.

- **Home Appliances and Kitchen Gadgets:** Kitchen appliances, cookware, and gadgets make cooking and meal preparation easier and more enjoyable for consumers.

**6. Travel and Tourism:**

- **Airline and Hotel Booking:** Travel affiliate programs offer commissions for bookings made through affiliate links, including flights, hotels, and vacation packages.

- **Travel Gear and Accessories:** Luggage, travel accessories, and outdoor gear are essential for travelers seeking comfort and convenience on their adventures.

- **Travel Guides and Experiences:** Travel guides, tours, and experiences cater to individuals seeking unique and memorable travel experiences around the world.

**7. Parenting and Family:**

- **Baby Care and Parenting Products:** Baby gear, parenting books, and childcare services are essential for new parents and families with young children.

- **Education and Child Development:** Educational toys, learning resources, and online courses cater to parents and caregivers seeking to support their children's growth and development.

- **Family Activities and Entertainment:** Family-friendly attractions, games, and activities provide opportunities for quality time and bonding among family members.

These are just a few examples of popular affiliate marketing niches that offer significant opportunities for monetization and growth. However, it's essential to conduct thorough research, evaluate market demand, and consider your interests and expertise when selecting a niche for your affiliate marketing business. By choosing a niche that resonates with your target audience and aligns with your goals, you can build a successful affiliate marketing business and achieve sustainable long-term success.

## How to Identify a Profitable Niche

Identifying a profitable niche is essential for the success of your affiliate marketing business.

**The steps to help you identify a niche with high potential for profitability:**

**1. Conduct Market Research:**
   - Use online tools like Google Trends, Keyword Planner, and niche research websites to analyze trends and search volume for potential niches.
   - Look for niches with consistent or growing demand over time, indicating sustained interest from consumers.

- Consider seasonal trends, market fluctuations, and emerging opportunities to identify niches with long-term potential.

**2. Assess Market Demand:**
- Evaluate the level of demand for products or services within your chosen niche.
- Look for niches with a large target audience and significant purchasing power, indicating a higher likelihood of generating sales and commissions.
- Explore related keywords, forums, social media groups, and online communities to gauge interest and engagement within the niche.

**3. Analyze Competition:**
- Assess the level of competition within your chosen niche to determine your ability to stand out and succeed.
- Look for niches with moderate to low competition, where you can differentiate yourself and offer unique value to your audience.
- Explore competitor websites, content, promotions, and strategies to identify gaps, weaknesses, and opportunities for improvement.

**4. Evaluate Monetization Opportunities:**

- Research affiliate programs, products, and services available within your chosen niche.
- Look for affiliate programs with attractive commission rates, recurring revenue opportunities, and high-converting products.
- Consider the diversity and quality of affiliate products available, as well as the reliability and reputation of affiliate networks or platforms.

**5. Understand Audience Needs and Pain Points:**

- Identify the needs, problems, and pain points of your target audience within the niche.
- Conduct surveys, interviews, or market research to gain insights into consumer preferences, challenges, and motivations.
- Look for niches where you can provide valuable solutions, recommendations, and content that addresses your audience's specific needs and desires.

**6. Consider Evergreen Appeal:**

- Choose a niche with evergreen appeal, meaning it has consistent demand and relevance over time.

- Avoid niches that are overly trendy or fads that may lose popularity quickly.

- Look for niches with enduring relevance and longevity, such as health and wellness, personal finance, or lifestyle topics.

**7. Assess Your Interests and Expertise:**

- Consider your own interests, passions, and expertise when selecting a niche.

- Choose a niche that aligns with your interests and knowledge, as this will make the process more enjoyable and sustainable.

- Leverage your expertise and experience to create valuable content, establish credibility, and connect with your audience authentically.

**8. Test and Validate Your Niche:**

- Start by creating a small-scale test or pilot project within your chosen niche to gauge its potential.

- Produce content, promote affiliate products, and engage with your audience to measure interest, engagement, and conversion rates.

- Monitor key metrics such as website traffic, email sign-ups, click-through rates, and sales to assess the viability and profitability of your niche.

Identifying a profitable niche requires careful research, analysis, and validation. By understanding market demand, competition, monetization opportunities, audience needs, and your own interests and expertise, you can choose a niche with high potential for profitability in affiliate marketing. Take the time to conduct thorough research, test and validate your niche, and iterate based on feedback and data insights to build a successful and sustainable affiliate marketing business.

## Tools for Niche Research

**Several tools can aid you in conducting niche research for your affiliate marketing business. Here are some popular ones:**

**1. Google Trends:**

- Provides insights into search trends and popularity for specific keywords or topics over time.

- Helps you identify rising trends, seasonal fluctuations, and regional interest in potential niches.

- Allows comparison of multiple keywords to assess relative search volume and interest.

**2. Google Keyword Planner:**

- Helps you discover relevant keywords and phrases related to your niche.

- Provides data on search volume, competition, and suggested bid prices for keywords.

- Useful for identifying high-value keywords and optimizing content for search engine optimization (SEO).

**3. Ahrefs:**

- Offers comprehensive SEO tools for keyword research, competitor analysis, and backlink analysis.

- Provides data on keyword difficulty, search volume, and traffic potential for specific keywords.

- Allows you to analyze competitor websites, backlink profiles, and top-performing content in your niche.

**4. Semrush:**

- Provides SEO and marketing analytics tools for keyword research, competitor analysis, and content optimization.

- Offers data on organic and paid search traffic, keyword rankings, and backlink profiles.

- Allows you to track competitors' marketing strategies, advertising campaigns, and performance metrics.

**5. Ubersuggest:**

- Offers keyword research tools, content ideas, and SEO insights for niche research.

- Provides data on search volume, keyword difficulty, and related keywords for specific niches.

- Helps you identify long-tail keywords, content gaps, and opportunities for optimization.

### 6. BuzzSumo:

- Helps you discover popular content and trending topics within your niche.

- Provides insights into social media engagement, shares, and backlinks for specific content pieces.

- Allows you to identify influential content creators and publishers in your niche.

### 7. AnswerThePublic:

- Generates a visual representation of commonly asked questions and search queries related to your niche.

- Provides insights into user intent, pain points, and interests within your niche.

- Helps you identify content ideas, FAQ topics, and keyword opportunities based on user queries.

### 8. Quora:

- A platform where users ask questions and share knowledge on various topics.

- Allows you to explore questions and discussions related to your niche to understand audience interests and concerns.

- Provides valuable insights into common problems, challenges, and interests within your niche.

**9. Reddit:**
 - A social news aggregation and discussion platform with niche-specific communities (subreddits).
 - Allows you to join relevant subreddits related to your niche and participate in discussions.
 - Provides insights into trending topics, popular content, and community interests within your niche.

**10. Facebook Audience Insights:**
 - Provides demographic and interest data on Facebook users related to your niche.
 - Helps you understand audience demographics, interests, and behaviors to tailor your marketing efforts.
 - Allows you to create targeted ad campaigns and reach specific audience segments within your niche.

These tools offer valuable insights and data to support your niche research efforts in affiliate marketing. By leveraging these tools effectively, you can identify profitable niches, understand audience interests and preferences, and optimize your marketing strategies for success. Experiment with different tools and methodologies to gather comprehensive data and make informed decisions when selecting a niche for your affiliate marketing business.

# Chapter 3: Finding and Joining Affiliate Programs

Joining affiliate programs is a crucial step in monetizing your affiliate marketing efforts. Here's a comprehensive guide on how to find and join affiliate programs effectively:

**1. Identify Relevant Affiliate Networks:**

 - Start by researching affiliate networks that specialize in your niche or industry.

 - Popular affiliate networks include ShareASale, CJ Affiliate (formerly Commission Junction), Amazon Associates, Rakuten Marketing, and ClickBank.

 - Consider factors such as the range of affiliate programs available, commission rates, payment terms, and network reputation when choosing affiliate networks.

**2. Search for Affiliate Programs:**

- Use the search or browse functions within affiliate networks to find relevant affiliate programs.

- Filter programs based on criteria such as niche, product type, commission structure, and payout frequency.

- Explore program details, including commission rates, cookie duration, promotional materials, and program terms, to assess suitability.

**3. Research Merchant Websites:**

- Visit merchant websites directly to explore their affiliate program offerings.

- Look for affiliate program information in the website footer, navigation menu, or dedicated affiliate program pages.

- Review program details, requirements, and benefits to determine if the merchant's affiliate program aligns with your interests and goals.

**4. Utilize Affiliate Program Directories:**

- Explore affiliate program directories and databases to discover a wide range of affiliate programs across different industries.

- Websites like Affilorama, Affi.io, and AffiliatePrograms.com offer directories of affiliate programs categorized by niche, industry, and network.

- Use advanced search filters to narrow down options based on specific criteria, such as commission rates, payout methods, and program features.

**5. Join Individual Affiliate Programs:**

- Once you've identified affiliate programs of interest, review their application and approval process.

- Complete the affiliate program application by providing accurate information about your website, traffic sources, promotional methods, and audience demographics.

- Some affiliate programs may require additional documentation or verification steps before approving your application.

**6. Read and Accept Program Terms:**

- Review the terms and conditions of each affiliate program carefully before joining.

- Pay attention to commission rates, cookie durations, payment thresholds, promotional guidelines, and prohibited activities.

- Ensure that you understand and agree to the program terms to avoid violations and potential account termination.

**7. Get Your Affiliate Links:**

- Upon approval into an affiliate program, access your affiliate dashboard or account to retrieve your unique affiliate tracking links.

- Generate affiliate links for specific products, pages, or promotions that you plan to promote.

- Customize affiliate links with tracking parameters to monitor performance and optimize your marketing campaigns.

**8. Access Promotional Materials:**

- Explore the affiliate dashboard or resources section to access promotional materials provided by the merchant.

- Download banners, text links, product images, and other creatives to use in your marketing campaigns.

- Leverage promotional materials to create compelling content and effectively promote affiliate products to your audience.

**9. Track and Monitor Performance:**

- Use tracking tools and analytics provided by affiliate networks or tracking software to monitor your affiliate performance.

- Track clicks, conversions, sales, commissions, and other key metrics to measure the effectiveness of your marketing efforts.

- Analyze performance data to identify top-performing products, campaigns, and strategies and optimize your affiliate marketing strategy accordingly.

**10. Comply with Program Policies:**

- Adhere to the terms and guidelines outlined in each affiliate program's policies and agreements.

- Avoid engaging in prohibited activities such as spamming, cookie stuffing, trademark bidding, or misleading advertising.

- Maintain transparency and integrity in your promotional efforts to build trust with your audience and affiliate partners.

Finding and joining affiliate programs is a foundational step in building a successful affiliate marketing business. By researching affiliate networks, exploring relevant programs, and following the application and approval process, you can access a diverse range of affiliate opportunities and monetize your online presence effectively. Remember to review program terms, access affiliate links and promotional materials, track performance, and comply with program policies to maximize your earning potential and foster long-term partnerships with affiliate merchants.

## Top Affiliate Networks to Join

Joining affiliate networks can provide access to a wide range of affiliate programs across various industries and niches. Here are some of the top affiliate networks that offer lucrative opportunities for affiliate marketers:

**1. ShareASale:**

- One of the largest and most established affiliate networks, offering thousands of affiliate programs in diverse niches.

- Features a user-friendly platform with advanced reporting tools, real-time tracking, and deep linking capabilities.

- Provides a wide range of affiliate programs with competitive commission rates and reliable payouts.

**2. CJ Affiliate (formerly Commission Junction):**

- A leading global affiliate marketing network with a vast network of advertisers and publishers.

- Offers a robust platform with advanced tracking technology, performance insights, and affiliate support services.

- Provides access to high-quality affiliate programs from top brands and advertisers across various industries.

**3. Amazon Associates:**

- The affiliate program of Amazon, the world's largest online retailer, offering a wide selection of products and categories.

- Features competitive commission rates, performance-based bonuses, and a trusted brand reputation.

- Provides access to millions of products for affiliate promotion, along with advanced tracking and reporting tools.

**4. Rakuten Marketing (formerly Rakuten Affiliate Network):**

- A global affiliate marketing network with a diverse range of advertisers and publishers.

- Offers a user-friendly platform with robust tracking, reporting, and optimization tools.

- Provides access to affiliate programs from leading brands and merchants across multiple verticals.

**5. ClickBank:**

- A popular affiliate network specializing in digital products, including e-books, courses, software, and digital downloads.

- Features a marketplace with thousands of affiliate programs in various niches, including health, fitness, self-help, and business.
- Offers high commission rates, recurring commissions, and customizable affiliate links for tracking and optimization.

**6. Impact (formerly Impact Radius):**
- A comprehensive affiliate marketing platform with a focus on performance-based partnerships.
- Offers advanced tracking and attribution capabilities, real-time reporting, and customizable commission structures.
- Provides access to affiliate programs from leading brands and advertisers in e-commerce, retail, travel, and more.

**7. FlexOffers:**
- A well-established affiliate network with thousands of affiliate programs across diverse verticals.
- Offers a user-friendly platform with advanced tracking, reporting, and optimization tools.

- Provides access to exclusive offers, promotional materials, and dedicated affiliate support services.

### 8. Awin:

- A global affiliate marketing network with a vast network of advertisers and publishers in over 180 countries.
- Offers a comprehensive platform with advanced tracking, reporting, and payment processing capabilities.
- Provides access to affiliate programs from top brands and merchants in fashion, beauty, technology, and other industries.

### 9. Pepperjam:

- An affiliate marketing platform offering innovative technology solutions and strategic partnerships.
- Features a robust platform with advanced tracking, reporting, and optimization tools.
- Provides access to affiliate programs from leading brands and advertisers, along with dedicated account management and support.

**10. Skimlinks:**

- A content monetization platform that automatically converts product links into affiliate links.

- Offers a seamless integration with publishers' content, allowing them to earn commissions from product recommendations.

- Provides access to a network of affiliate programs from thousands of merchants, simplifying the affiliate marketing process for publishers.

These top affiliate networks offer diverse opportunities for affiliate marketers to join high-quality affiliate programs, access advanced tools and resources, and monetize their online presence effectively. Whether you're a beginner or experienced affiliate marketer, exploring these affiliate networks can help you discover new opportunities, expand your reach, and maximize your earning potential in the affiliate marketing industry.

# Evaluating Affiliate Programs

Evaluating affiliate programs is essential to ensure that you partner with reputable merchants and maximize your earning potential.

**The key factors to consider when evaluating affiliate programs:**

**1. Commission Structure:**

   - **Commission Rates:** Consider the commission rates offered by the affiliate program. Look for programs that offer competitive commission rates relative to the industry average.

   - **Recurring Commissions:** Determine if the program offers recurring commissions for ongoing sales or subscriptions. Recurring commissions can lead to passive income streams over time.

   - **Performance Bonuses:** Some affiliate programs offer performance-based bonuses or incentives for achieving specific sales targets or milestones. Evaluate the bonus structure and eligibility criteria for additional earning opportunities.

**2. Cookie Duration:**

- **Cookie Length:** Assess the cookie duration provided by the affiliate program. A longer cookie duration allows you to earn commissions on sales made by referred customers within the cookie window.

- **Multi-device Tracking:** Ensure that the affiliate program supports multi-device tracking to track sales across different devices and browsers. This ensures that you receive credit for sales generated by your referrals, regardless of the device used.

**3. Product Quality and Relevance:**

- **Product Quality:** Evaluate the quality and relevance of the products or services offered by the merchant. Partner with merchants that offer high-quality products or services that align with your audience's interests and needs.

- **Brand Reputation:** Consider the reputation and credibility of the merchant's brand. Partnering with reputable brands enhances your credibility as an affiliate and increases the likelihood of conversion.

**4. Affiliate Support and Resources:**

- **Promotional Materials:** Assess the availability of promotional materials provided by the affiliate program, such as banners, text links, product images, and landing pages. Access to high-quality promotional materials can facilitate your marketing efforts.

- **Dedicated Support:** Determine if the affiliate program offers dedicated support services for affiliates, such as account managers or support representatives. Responsive support can help address inquiries, resolve issues, and optimize your affiliate marketing strategy.

**5. Tracking and Reporting:**

- **Tracking Accuracy:** Ensure that the affiliate program utilizes reliable tracking technology to accurately track clicks, sales, and commissions. Look for features such as pixel tracking, server-to-server tracking, and cookie-based tracking for accurate attribution.

- **Real-time Reporting:** Evaluate the availability of real-time reporting and analytics tools provided by the affiliate program. Access to performance data allows you to monitor your affiliate activities, track key metrics, and optimize your campaigns for better results.

**6. Payment Terms:**

- **Payment Threshold:** Determine the payment threshold required to receive affiliate commissions. Some programs have a minimum payment threshold that must be reached before payouts are issued.

- **Payment Frequency:** Assess the payment frequency offered by the affiliate program, such as monthly, bi-weekly, or weekly payouts. Choose programs with regular payment schedules that align with your cash flow needs.

**7. Program Policies and Terms:**

- **Promotional Guidelines:** Review the program's promotional guidelines and terms of service to ensure compliance with their policies. Avoid engaging in prohibited activities such as spamming, incentivized traffic, or trademark bidding.

- **Terms of Service:** Read and understand the program's terms of service, including commission structures, payout terms, and termination clauses. Ensure that you agree with the terms before joining the affiliate program.

## 8. User Experience and Conversion Rate:

- **Merchant Website:** Evaluate the user experience and conversion rate of the merchant's website. A well-designed and optimized website can lead to higher conversion rates and increased earnings for affiliates.

- **Conversion Rate Optimization:** Consider if the merchant implements conversion rate optimization (CRO) strategies to improve the likelihood of conversion. Look for features such as A/B testing, optimized landing pages, and clear calls-to-action (CTAs).

Evaluating affiliate programs requires careful consideration of commission structure, cookie duration, product quality, affiliate support, tracking and reporting, payment terms, program policies, user experience, and conversion rate. By assessing these factors, you can select affiliate programs that offer competitive commissions, quality products, reliable tracking, and favorable terms, maximizing your earning potential as an affiliate marketer.

# How to Sign Up and Get Approved

Signing up and getting approved for affiliate programs involves several steps to ensure that you meet the program's requirements and guidelines.

**The guide on how to sign up and get approved for affiliate programs:**

**1. Research Affiliate Programs:**
   - Identify affiliate programs that align with your niche, audience, and marketing goals.
   - Research program details, including commission rates, cookie duration, product offerings, and promotional materials.

**2. Visit the Merchant's Website or Affiliate Network:**

- Visit the merchant's website directly or access the affiliate program through an affiliate network.

- Navigate to the affiliate program section or look for affiliate program information on the merchant's website.

### 3. Complete the Application:

- Fill out the affiliate program application form with accurate information.

- Provide details about your website or marketing channels, traffic sources, promotional methods, and audience demographics.

### 4. Provide Additional Information:

- Some affiliate programs may require additional documentation or verification steps to approve your application.

- Be prepared to provide supplementary information such as your contact details, tax ID or social security number (for tax purposes), and payment preferences.

### 5. Review Program Terms and Conditions:

- Read and understand the program's terms and conditions, including commission structures, payout terms, promotional guidelines, and prohibited activities.

- Ensure that you agree with the terms before submitting your application.

**6. Wait for Approval:**

- After submitting your application, wait for the affiliate program to review and approve your application.

- Approval times may vary depending on the program's review process and workload. Be patient and avoid contacting the program repeatedly for updates.

**7. Follow Up if Necessary:**

- If you haven't received a response within a reasonable timeframe, you can follow up with the affiliate program to inquire about the status of your application.

- Send a polite email or message requesting an update on your application status and expressing your interest in joining the program.

**8. Receive Approval Notification:**

- Once your application is approved, you will receive a notification from the affiliate program confirming your acceptance.

- The notification may include instructions on how to access your affiliate dashboard, generate affiliate links, and access promotional materials.

**9. Access Affiliate Dashboard:**

- Log in to your affiliate dashboard or account to access affiliate resources, tracking tools, and promotional materials.

- Familiarize yourself with the dashboard layout and navigation to effectively manage your affiliate activities.

**10. Start Promoting:**

- Begin promoting affiliate products or services using your unique affiliate links provided by the program.

- Create compelling content, optimize your marketing channels, and engage with your audience to drive traffic and conversions.

Signing up and getting approved for affiliate programs involves completing the application process, providing accurate information, reviewing program terms, and waiting for approval. By following these steps and adhering to program guidelines, you can increase your chances of being accepted into affiliate programs and start earning commissions as an affiliate marketer.

## Understanding Commission Structures

Understanding commission structures is essential for affiliate marketers to maximize their earnings and optimize their affiliate marketing strategies.

**The overview of common commission structures used in affiliate programs:**

**1. Percentage-Based Commission:**
Affiliates earn a percentage of the sale amount for each successful referral they generate.

- **Example:** A program offers a 10% commission rate, and a customer makes a $100 purchase through an affiliate link. The affiliate earns $10 in commission (10% of $100).

**2. Fixed Commission:**
Affiliates earn a fixed amount for each successful referral, regardless of the sale amount.
- **Example:** A program offers a $20 commission for every referral that results in a sale. Regardless of the purchase value, the affiliate earns $20 for each successful referral.

**3. Tiered Commission:**
Affiliates earn different commission rates based on predefined sales tiers or thresholds.
- **Example:** A program offers tiered commissions as follows: 5% for sales up to $500, 7% for sales between $501 and $1000, and 10% for sales exceeding $1000. Affiliates earn commission rates based on the corresponding sales tiers.

**4. Performance-Based Commission:**

Affiliates earn commissions based on their performance or achievements, such as the number of sales, leads, or conversions generated.

   - **Example:** A program offers performance-based bonuses, such as a $100 bonus for every 100 sales generated within a month. Affiliates can earn additional commissions based on their performance metrics.

**5. Recurring Commission:**

Affiliates earn commissions on recurring purchases or subscriptions made by referred customers over time.

   - **Example:** A program offers a 20% recurring commission for subscription-based products or services. Affiliates earn commissions each time the customer renews their subscription.

**6. Hybrid Commission:**

Affiliates earn a combination of fixed and percentage-based commissions or a mix of different commission structures.

   - **Example:** A program offers a $10 fixed commission plus a 5% commission on the sale amount. Affiliates earn both the fixed amount and a percentage of the sale value.

## 7. CPA (Cost-Per-Action) or CPL (Cost-Per-Lead) Commission:

Affiliates earn commissions for specific actions or conversions, such as sign-ups, form submissions, or free trial registrations.

- **Example:** A program offers a $5 commission for every email sign-up generated through an affiliate link. Affiliates earn commissions for each successful action completed by referred users.

## 8. CPM (Cost-Per-Mille) or CPC (Cost-Per-Click) Commission:

Affiliates earn commissions based on the number of impressions (CPM) or clicks (CPC) generated by their referral links or promotional materials.

- **Example:** A program offers a $1 commission for every 1000 ad impressions (CPM) or every click (CPC) on an affiliate banner ad. Affiliates earn commissions based on the volume of impressions or clicks generated.

Understanding commission structures is crucial for affiliate marketers to assess earning potential, select lucrative affiliate programs, and optimize their marketing efforts. By familiarizing themselves with different commission models and evaluating program terms, affiliates can effectively monetize their traffic and maximize their earnings in affiliate marketing.

# Chapter 4: Building Your Platform

Building your platform is a foundational step in establishing a successful affiliate marketing business. Your platform serves as the primary channel through which you engage with your audience, promote affiliate products, and drive traffic to merchant websites.

**Here's a comprehensive guide on how to build your platform effectively:**

**1. Define Your Audience and Niche:**

- **Audience Research:** Identify your target audience's demographics, interests, preferences, and pain points.

- **Niche Selection:** Choose a specific niche or topic that resonates with your audience and aligns with your expertise and interests.

**2. Choose Your Platform:**

**- Website:** Create a blog or website to serve as your central hub for content creation, promotion, and affiliate marketing.

   **- Social Media:** Leverage social media platforms such as Instagram, YouTube, Facebook, or Pinterest to reach and engage with your audience.

   **- Email List:** Build an email list to nurture relationships with your audience, promote affiliate products, and drive conversions.

**3. Create High-Quality Content:**

   **- Content Strategy:** Develop a content strategy that addresses your audience's needs, interests, and pain points.

   **- Content Formats:** Produce diverse content formats such as blog posts, articles, videos, podcasts, infographics, and social media posts.

   **- Value Proposition:** Provide valuable, informative, and engaging content that educates, entertains, or solves problems for your audience.

**4. Optimize for Search Engines (SEO):**

- **Keyword Research:** Conduct keyword research to identify relevant keywords and phrases for your niche.

- **On-Page Optimization:** Optimize your website or content for search engines by incorporating targeted keywords, meta tags, headings, and internal links.

- **Quality Backlinks:** Build high-quality backlinks from reputable websites to improve your site's authority and visibility in search engine results.

### 5. Build Your Audience:

- **Engagement Strategies:** Engage with your audience through comments, social media interactions, live streams, webinars, and community forums.

- **Networking:** Collaborate with influencers, experts, and other content creators in your niche to expand your reach and audience.

- **Consistency:** Maintain a consistent publishing schedule and communication frequency to keep your audience engaged and informed.

### 6. Monetize Your Platform:

- **Affiliate Marketing:** Integrate affiliate links and promotions seamlessly into your content, recommendations, and product reviews.

- **Ad Revenue:** Generate revenue through display ads, sponsored content, or ad networks such as Google AdSense.

- **Digital Products:** Create and sell digital products such as e-books, courses, templates, or software related to your niche.

- **Membership/Subscriptions:** Offer premium content, exclusive access, or membership subscriptions for additional revenue streams.

**7. Analyze and Optimize Performance:**

- **Tracking Tools:** Use analytics tools such as Google Analytics, social media insights, and affiliate tracking platforms to monitor your platform's performance.

- **Metrics:** Track key metrics such as website traffic, engagement, conversion rates, click-through rates (CTRs), and affiliate earnings.

- **Optimization:** Continuously analyze data, identify trends, and optimize your content, marketing strategies, and monetization efforts for better results.

**8. Build Trust and Authority:**

- **Transparency:** Be transparent and honest with your audience about affiliate partnerships, sponsored content, and promotional relationships.

- **Quality and Integrity:** Maintain high standards of quality, integrity, and authenticity in your content, recommendations, and promotions.

- **Expertise:** Position yourself as an authority in your niche by sharing valuable insights, expertise, and unique perspectives with your audience.

Building your platform requires careful planning, consistent effort, and a focus on providing value to your audience. By defining your audience, creating high-quality content, optimizing for search engines, building your audience, monetizing effectively, analyzing performance, and building trust and authority, you can establish a successful platform for affiliate marketing and achieve sustainable long-term growth.

# Creating a Website or Blog

Creating a website or blog is an essential step in building your platform for affiliate marketing. Your website serves as the central hub for your content, promotions, and affiliate links.

**step-by-step guide on how to create a website or blog for affiliate marketing:**

**### 1. Choose a Domain Name and Hosting Provider:**
  - **Domain Name:** Select a domain name that reflects your brand, niche, or topic of interest. Choose a memorable, relevant, and easy-to-spell domain name.
  - **Hosting Provider:** Choose a reliable hosting provider that offers features such as security, speed, uptime guarantee, customer support, and scalability.

**2. Select a Content Management System (CMS):**

- **WordPress:** Consider using WordPress, the most popular CMS platform, for its flexibility, customization options, and extensive plugin ecosystem.

- **Other Options:** Explore alternative CMS platforms such as Wix, Squarespace, Joomla, or Drupal based on your preferences and technical requirements.

3. **Install and Set Up Your Website:**

- **Install WordPress:** Install WordPress on your hosting server using one-click installation tools provided by your hosting provider.

- **Configure Settings:** Set up basic settings such as site title, tagline, permalink structure, and timezone in the WordPress dashboard.

- **Choose a Theme:** Select a responsive and SEO-friendly WordPress theme that suits your niche, branding, and design preferences.

4. **Customize Your Website:**

- **Customize Theme:** Customize your chosen WordPress theme by adjusting colors, fonts, layouts, and other design elements to align with your brand identity.

- **Add Essential Pages:** Create essential pages such as Home, About, Contact, and Privacy Policy pages to provide important information and enhance user experience.

- **Install Plugins:** Install and activate essential plugins for functionality such as SEO optimization, security, caching, contact forms, and social media integration.

**5. Create Compelling Content:**

- **Content Strategy:** Develop a content strategy that addresses your audience's needs, interests, and pain points. Plan out your content calendar and topics in advance.

- **Create Quality Content:** Produce high-quality, informative, and engaging content such as blog posts, articles, tutorials, product reviews, and videos.

- **Optimize for SEO:** Optimize your content for search engines by incorporating relevant keywords, headings, meta tags, and internal links.

**6. Implement Affiliate Links and Promotions:**

- **Join Affiliate Programs:** Sign up for affiliate programs relevant to your niche and audience. Choose reputable merchants with high-quality products or services.

- **Insert Affiliate Links:** Integrate affiliate links seamlessly into your content, product reviews, recommendations, and call-to-action (CTA) buttons.

- **Disclose Affiliate Relationships:** Disclose your affiliate relationships clearly and transparently to your audience to maintain trust and compliance with regulations.

**7. Promote Your Website:**

- **Social Media:** Share your content and affiliate promotions on social media platforms such as Facebook, Twitter, Instagram, LinkedIn, and Pinterest.

- **Email Marketing:** Build an email list and send regular newsletters with valuable content, product recommendations, and affiliate promotions to your subscribers.

- **SEO and Link Building:** Optimize your website for search engines to improve visibility and organic traffic. Build backlinks from reputable websites to enhance your site's authority and ranking.

**8. Monitor and Analyze Performance:**

- **Analytics Tools:** Use website analytics tools such as Google Analytics to track key metrics such as traffic, engagement, conversion rates, and affiliate earnings.

- **Performance Optimization:** Analyze data insights to identify areas for improvement and optimize your content, marketing strategies, and monetization efforts for better results.

**9. Regularly Update and Maintain Your Website:**

- **Content Updates:** Publish fresh, relevant, and up-to-date content regularly to keep your audience engaged and attract new visitors.

- **Security and Maintenance:** Keep your website secure and up-to-date by installing security plugins, updating themes and plugins, and regularly backing up your site's data.

Creating a website or blog for affiliate marketing involves selecting a domain name, choosing a hosting provider, setting up your website, customizing your design, creating compelling content, integrating affiliate links, promoting your website, monitoring performance, and maintaining your site regularly. By following these steps and best practices, you can build a professional and effective platform to promote affiliate products, engage with your audience, and grow your affiliate marketing business.

## Leveraging Social Media for Affiliate Marketing

Leveraging social media for affiliate marketing can significantly expand your reach, engage with your audience, and drive traffic to affiliate products or services.

**The step-by-step guide on how to effectively utilize social media for affiliate marketing:**

**1. Choose the Right Social Media Platforms:**

- Identify social media platforms that align with your target audience, niche, and content format preferences.

- Consider popular platforms such as Instagram, YouTube, Facebook, Twitter, LinkedIn, Pinterest, TikTok, or Snapchat.

**2. Optimize Your Social Media Profiles:**

- Create and optimize your social media profiles with relevant keywords, engaging descriptions, and branded visuals.

- Include a clear and compelling bio or description that highlights your niche, expertise, and affiliate partnerships.

- Add links to your website, blog, or landing pages where you promote affiliate products or services.

**3. Develop a Content Strategy:**

- Define your content strategy based on your audience's interests, preferences, and pain points.

- Plan out content themes, topics, formats, and posting schedules to maintain consistency and engagement.

- Mix promotional content with valuable, informative, and entertaining content to provide value to your audience.

**4. Create Engaging Content:**
- Produce high-quality, visually appealing content such as photos, videos, stories, reels, live streams, or infographics.
- Craft compelling captions, descriptions, and calls-to-action (CTAs) that encourage engagement, clicks, and conversions.
- Use storytelling, humor, personal anecdotes, or user-generated content to captivate your audience and build trust.

**5. Integrate Affiliate Links and Promotions:**
- Join affiliate programs relevant to your niche and audience. Choose merchants with products or services that align with your audience's interests and needs.
- Integrate affiliate links seamlessly into your social media content, posts, captions, and bio where appropriate.

- Disclose your affiliate relationships transparently and comply with platform guidelines and regulations regarding affiliate marketing.

**6. Engage with Your Audience:**

- Foster meaningful interactions with your audience by responding to comments, messages, and mentions promptly.
- Encourage user-generated content (UGC), feedback, reviews, and testimonials to increase engagement and social proof.
- Host Q&A sessions, polls, contests, or live streams to encourage participation and build community around your brand.

**7. Collaborate with Influencers and Partners:**

- Collaborate with influencers, content creators, or brands in your niche to amplify your reach and exposure.
- Partner with influencers or affiliates to co-create content, host joint giveaways, or cross-promote each other's products or services.

- Leverage influencer marketing platforms or networks to discover potential collaborators and streamline partnership processes.

**8. Track Performance and Analytics:**

- Use social media analytics tools and built-in insights to track key metrics such as reach, engagement, clicks, conversions, and affiliate earnings.

- Analyze data insights to understand what types of content resonate with your audience, which platforms drive the most traffic and conversions, and optimize your social media strategy accordingly.

**9. Stay Updated and Adapt:**

- Stay informed about social media trends, algorithm changes, platform updates, and best practices for affiliate marketing.

- Experiment with new content formats, features, and strategies to stay relevant and adapt to evolving audience preferences and platform dynamics.

Leveraging social media for affiliate marketing requires strategic planning, engaging content creation, transparent promotion, active engagement, collaborative partnerships, performance tracking, and continuous adaptation. With these steps and best practices, you can effectively leverage social media platforms to promote affiliate products, grow your audience, and generate revenue as an affiliate marketer.

## Email Marketing for Affiliates

Email marketing is a powerful tool for affiliate marketers to nurture relationships with their audience, promote affiliate products, and drive conversions.

**The comprehensive guide on how to effectively utilize email marketing for affiliate marketing:**

**1. Build an Email List:**
  - **Opt-in Forms:** Place opt-in forms strategically on your website, blog, or social media profiles to encourage visitors to subscribe to your email list.

- **Lead Magnets:** Offer valuable incentives such as e-books, guides, checklists, or exclusive content in exchange for email subscriptions.

- **Popup Forms:** Use exit-intent popups, slide-ins, or lightbox forms to capture visitors' attention and prompt them to subscribe before leaving your site.

## 2. Segment Your Email List:

- **Audience Segmentation:** Segment your email list based on demographics, interests, behavior, or engagement level to send targeted and personalized emails.

- **Custom Fields:** Collect additional information from subscribers using custom fields to tailor your email content and promotions to their preferences.

## 3. Craft Compelling Email Content:

- **Welcome Series:** Send a series of welcome emails to new subscribers to introduce yourself, set expectations, and deliver value.

- **Content Updates:** Share valuable content such as blog posts, articles, videos, or podcasts related to your niche to educate, entertain, or inspire your subscribers.

- **Product Recommendations:** Promote affiliate products or services through product reviews, recommendations, tutorials, or exclusive offers tailored to your audience's interests.

- **Exclusive Deals:** Offer exclusive discounts, promotions, or bonuses to your email subscribers to incentivize purchases and drive conversions.

**4. Optimize Email Design and Copy:**

- **Responsive Design:** Ensure that your emails are mobile-friendly and optimized for various devices and screen sizes to maximize readability and engagement.

- **Clear CTAs:** Include clear and compelling calls-to-action (CTAs) that prompt subscribers to take action, such as clicking on affiliate links or making a purchase.

- **Engaging Copy:** Write concise, persuasive, and engaging copy that highlights the benefits, features, and value propositions of the affiliate products or services you're promoting.

## 5. Personalize Email Campaigns:

- **Personalization Tokens:** Use merge tags or personalization tokens to dynamically insert subscribers' names, locations, or past purchase history into your emails for a personalized touch.

- **Behavioral Triggers:** Set up automated email sequences triggered by specific actions or behaviors, such as abandoned cart reminders, product recommendations, or re-engagement emails.

## 6. Test and Optimize:

- **A/B Testing:** Experiment with different subject lines, email copy, design elements, and CTAs through A/B testing to identify what resonates best with your audience.

- **Performance Tracking:** Track key metrics such as open rates, click-through rates (CTRs), conversion rates, and affiliate earnings to measure the effectiveness of your email campaigns.

- **Iterative Improvements:** Continuously analyze data insights, iterate on your email content and strategies, and optimize your campaigns based on performance results.

**7. Maintain Compliance and Transparency:**

- **Compliance:** Ensure compliance with email marketing regulations such as the CAN-SPAM Act by including unsubscribe links, providing clear sender information, and honoring subscribers' preferences.

- **Disclosure:** Disclose your affiliate relationships transparently in your email content and promotions to maintain trust and compliance with regulatory requirements.

**8. Provide Value and Nurture Relationships:**

- **Value-Driven Approach:** Focus on providing value to your email subscribers by delivering relevant, helpful, and actionable content that addresses their needs and interests.

- **Relationship Building:** Foster genuine relationships with your subscribers by engaging with them, responding to their inquiries, and soliciting feedback to understand their preferences and challenges better.

**9. Collaborate with Affiliate Programs and Partners:**

- **Affiliate Promotions:** Partner with affiliate programs and merchants to access exclusive deals, promotions, or affiliate incentives to offer to your email subscribers.

- **Joint Ventures:** Collaborate with other affiliates or brands in your niche to cross-promote each other's products or services to your respective email lists.

**10. Stay Consistent and Engaged:**

- **Consistency:** Maintain a consistent email cadence and frequency to stay top-of-mind with your subscribers and reinforce your brand presence.

- **Engagement:** Encourage interaction and feedback from your subscribers through surveys, polls, quizzes, or interactive content to enhance engagement and loyalty.

Email marketing is a valuable tool for affiliate marketers to nurture relationships, promote affiliate products, and drive conversions. By building an email list, segmenting your audience, crafting compelling content, optimizing design and copy, personalizing campaigns, testing and optimizing, maintaining compliance and transparency, providing value, nurturing relationships, collaborating with affiliate programs and partners, and staying consistent and engaged, you can leverage email marketing effectively to grow your affiliate marketing business and generate revenue.

## Content Creation Strategies

Content creation is at the heart of affiliate marketing, serving as the vehicle through which you provide value to your audience and promote affiliate products or services.

**Here are some effective content creation strategies for affiliate marketers:**

**1. Understand Your Audience:**
   - **Audience Research:** Conduct thorough research to understand your target audience's

demographics, interests, preferences, and pain points.

- **Buyer Personas:** Create detailed buyer personas to represent different segments of your audience and tailor your content to their specific needs.

## 2. Provide Valuable Content:

- **Educational Content:** Create informative, instructional, or tutorial content that addresses your audience's questions, challenges, or learning objectives.

- **Entertaining Content:** Produce entertaining, engaging, or inspirational content that captivates your audience's attention and fosters emotional connections.

- **Problem-Solving Content:** Offer solutions, tips, strategies, or actionable advice to help your audience overcome common challenges or achieve their goals.

## 3. Choose Relevant Topics:

- **Keyword Research:** Conduct keyword research to identify relevant topics, trends, and search queries related to your niche or industry.

- **Trending Topics:** Stay updated on industry trends, news, and developments to create timely and relevant content that resonates with your audience.

**4. Diversify Content Formats:**

- **Blog Posts:** Write informative articles, guides, listicles, or how-to posts that provide valuable insights and information to your audience.

- **Videos:** Produce video content such as tutorials, product reviews, demonstrations, or vlogs to engage visual learners and enhance engagement.

- **Podcasts:** Host podcasts or audio content where you discuss relevant topics, interview experts, or share insights with your audience.

- **Infographics:** Create visually appealing infographics or visual summaries to present complex information in a digestible format.

**5. Incorporate Affiliate Links Naturally:**

- **Contextual Integration:** Integrate affiliate links naturally within your content, recommendations, product reviews, or tutorials.

- **Relevancy:** Ensure that affiliate products or services you promote are relevant and aligned with the topic or theme of your content to enhance credibility and engagement.

- **Transparency:** Disclose your affiliate relationships transparently to your audience to maintain trust and compliance with regulations.

## 6. Optimize for SEO:

- **Keyword Optimization:** Optimize your content for relevant keywords, phrases, and long-tail search queries to improve visibility and search engine rankings.

- **On-Page SEO:** Optimize meta titles, descriptions, headings, and image alt text to enhance organic visibility and click-through rates (CTRs).

- **Quality Backlinks:** Build high-quality backlinks from reputable websites and sources within your niche to increase domain authority and referral traffic.

**7. Engage with Your Audience:**

- **Comments and Feedback:** Encourage audience engagement by responding to comments, questions, and feedback on your content or social media platforms.

- **Community Building:** Foster a sense of community by creating discussion forums, social media groups, or online communities where your audience can connect and interact with each other.

**8. Analyze Performance and Iterate:**

- **Data Insights:** Use analytics tools to track key metrics such as website traffic, engagement, conversion rates, and affiliate earnings.

- **Iterative Improvements:** Analyze data insights to identify trends, patterns, and areas for improvement, and iterate on your content strategy accordingly.

**9. Collaborate with Influencers and Experts:**

- **Influencer Collaborations:** Partner with influencers, experts, or industry leaders in your niche to co-create content, share audiences, or amplify your reach.

- **Guest Contributions:** Invite guest contributors or experts to contribute guest posts, interviews, or expert insights to provide additional value to your audience.

**10. Stay Consistent and Authentic:**

- **Consistency:** Maintain a consistent publishing schedule and content cadence to keep your audience engaged and reinforce your brand presence.

- **Authenticity:** Stay true to your brand voice, values, and personality to build trust and credibility with your audience over time.

Effective content creation is essential for affiliate marketers to provide value to their audience, promote affiliate products, and drive conversions. By understanding your audience, providing valuable content, choosing relevant topics, diversifying content formats, incorporating affiliate links naturally, optimizing for SEO, engaging with your audience, analyzing performance, iterating on your strategy, collaborating with influencers and experts, and staying consistent and authentic, you can create compelling content that resonates with your audience and contributes to the success of your affiliate marketing efforts.

# Chapter 5: Traffic Generation Strategies

Traffic generation is crucial for the success of any affiliate marketing venture.

**Here are some effective strategies to drive traffic to your affiliate offers:**

**1. Search Engine Optimization (SEO):**
  - **Keyword Research:** Identify relevant keywords and phrases related to your niche and target audience.
  - **On-Page SEO:** Optimize your website's meta tags, headings, content, and images for target keywords.
  - **Off-Page SEO:** Build high-quality backlinks from reputable websites to improve your site's authority and search engine rankings.

**2. Content Marketing:**
  - **Quality Content Creation:** Produce informative, engaging, and valuable content such

as blog posts, articles, videos, infographics, and podcasts.

- **Content Distribution:** Share your content on social media platforms, forums, communities, and content aggregation sites to reach a wider audience.

- **Guest Blogging:** Contribute guest posts to authoritative websites in your niche to expand your reach and build backlinks to your site.

**3. Social Media Marketing:**

- **Platform Selection:** Identify the social media platforms where your target audience is most active and engage with them effectively.

- **Content Sharing:** Share your content, affiliate promotions, and valuable insights on social media platforms such as Facebook, Instagram, Twitter, LinkedIn, Pinterest, and TikTok.

- **Engagement:** Interact with your audience by responding to comments, messages, and mentions, and participate in relevant discussions and communities.

**4. Email Marketing:**

- **Building an Email List:** Collect email addresses from your website visitors using opt-in forms, lead magnets, and incentives.

- **Newsletter Campaigns:** Send regular newsletters to your email subscribers with valuable content, promotions, and affiliate offers.

- **Segmentation:** Segment your email list based on demographics, interests, or engagement level to personalize your email campaigns and increase effectiveness.

## 5. Influencer Marketing:

- **Collaborate with Influencers:** Partner with influencers, bloggers, vloggers, or social media personalities in your niche to promote your affiliate offers to their audience.

- **Sponsored Content:** Sponsor influencer-created content such as reviews, tutorials, or endorsements featuring your affiliate products or services.

- **Affiliate Partnerships:** Offer influencers affiliate commissions or incentives for driving traffic and sales through their referral links.

### 6. Paid Advertising:

- **Google Ads:** Run pay-per-click (PPC) campaigns on Google Ads to target specific keywords and audience segments related to your affiliate offers.

- **Social Media Ads:** Utilize paid advertising options on social media platforms such as Facebook Ads, Instagram Ads, Twitter Ads, and LinkedIn Ads to reach your target audience.

- **Native Advertising:** Explore native advertising platforms and networks to promote your affiliate offers through sponsored content on relevant websites and media outlets.

### 7. Webinars and Events:

- **Host Webinars:** Organize educational or promotional webinars to engage with your audience, demonstrate products, and promote affiliate offers.

- **Attend Industry Events:** Participate in virtual or in-person industry events, conferences, or trade shows to network with peers, build relationships, and promote your affiliate business.

## 8. Referral Programs:

- **Incentivize Referrals:** Offer incentives or rewards to existing customers or affiliates for referring new customers or affiliates to your affiliate program.

- **Affiliate Networks:** Join affiliate networks or referral programs to leverage their existing networks and connections for traffic generation and lead generation.

## 9. Search Engine Marketing (SEM):

- **Pay-Per-Click (PPC) Advertising:** Bid on relevant keywords and phrases on search engines such as Google to display targeted ads for your affiliate offers.

- **Display Advertising:** Utilize display advertising networks and platforms to place visual ads on websites, blogs, and apps frequented by your target audience.

## 10. Analytics and Optimization:

- **Track Performance:** Monitor key metrics such as website traffic, click-through rates (CTRs), conversion rates, and affiliate earnings using analytics tools.

- **Optimize Campaigns:** Analyze data insights to identify trends, optimize your traffic generation strategies, and allocate resources effectively to maximize ROI.

Implementing a combination of these traffic generation strategies can help you attract targeted traffic to your affiliate offers, increase conversions, and maximize your affiliate marketing revenue. Experiment with different tactics, measure your results, and continuously refine your approach to achieve long-term success in affiliate marketing.

## SEO Basics for Affiliate Marketers

SEO (Search Engine Optimization) is essential for affiliate marketers to improve their website's visibility in search engine results pages (SERPs) and attract organic traffic.

**The basic SEO strategies tailored for affiliate marketers:**

**1. Keyword Research:**

   - **Identify Relevant Keywords:** Research keywords and phrases related to your niche, products, and target audience using tools like Google Keyword Planner, SEMrush, or Ahrefs.

   - **Long-Tail Keywords:** Target long-tail keywords that have lower competition and higher intent, focusing on specific topics or queries relevant to your affiliate offers.

   - **Competitor Analysis:** Analyze competitors' keywords and content strategies to identify opportunities and gaps in your own SEO approach.

**2. On-Page Optimization:**

   - **Title Tags:** Optimize title tags to include relevant keywords and entice users to click, keeping them concise (around 60 characters) and compelling.

   - **Meta Descriptions:** Write persuasive meta descriptions that summarize your content and encourage clicks, also incorporating keywords naturally.

- **Header Tags:** Use header tags (H1, H2, H3, etc.) to structure your content logically and include target keywords in headings where appropriate.

- **Keyword Placement:** Incorporate keywords naturally throughout your content, including in the URL, headings, body text, and image alt attributes.

- **Internal Linking:** Link internally to other relevant pages on your website to improve navigation, distribute link equity, and enhance user experience.

**3. Quality Content Creation:**

- **Valuable Content:** Create high-quality, informative, and engaging content that addresses user intent and provides solutions to their queries or problems.

- **Originality:** Aim for original, unique content that adds value and distinguishes your website from competitors, avoiding duplicate or thin content.

- **Keyword Density:** Maintain a natural keyword density in your content, avoiding keyword stuffing and focusing on readability and user experience.

- **Content Updates:** Regularly update and refresh your content to keep it relevant, accurate, and in line with current search trends and algorithms.

**4. Mobile Optimization:**

- **Responsive Design:** Ensure your website is mobile-friendly and responsive, providing a seamless user experience across different devices and screen sizes.

- **Page Speed:** Optimize page speed by minimizing server response times, leveraging browser caching, compressing images, and reducing unnecessary code.

- **Mobile Usability:** Check and improve mobile usability factors such as font size, tap targets, and viewport configuration to enhance mobile user experience.

**5. Link Building:**

- **Quality Backlinks:** Focus on acquiring high-quality backlinks from authoritative websites, relevant directories, industry publications, and niche influencers.

- **Natural Link Building:** Foster natural link building through valuable content, outreach, guest blogging, and relationship building rather than manipulative tactics.

- **Anchor Text Optimization:** Use descriptive and relevant anchor text for your backlinks, incorporating target keywords where appropriate to enhance relevance and SEO value.

### 6. Technical SEO:

- **Site Structure:** Optimize your site's structure and navigation for both users and search engines, ensuring a logical hierarchy and easy crawlability.

- **XML Sitemap:** Create and submit an XML sitemap to search engines to help them discover and index your website's pages more efficiently.

- **Robots.txt:** Use a robots.txt file to control search engine crawlers' access to specific pages or directories on your website, improving crawl efficiency and indexation.

### 7. User Experience (UX):

- **Intuitive Design:** Design your website with a focus on usability, clarity, and intuitiveness to provide a positive user experience and encourage engagement.

- **Clear Call-to-Actions (CTAs):** Include clear and compelling CTAs throughout your website to guide users towards desired actions, such as signing up, subscribing, or making a purchase.

- **Mobile Optimization:** Prioritize mobile optimization to ensure seamless navigation and interaction for mobile users, optimizing layouts, buttons, and forms accordingly.

**8. Analytics and Monitoring:**

- **Google Analytics:** Set up Google Analytics to track and analyze website traffic, user behavior, conversions, and other key metrics, gaining insights into your SEO performance.

- **Search Console:** Use Google Search Console to monitor your website's presence in search results, identify indexing issues, and receive alerts about potential SEO issues.

Implementing these SEO basics, affiliate marketers can enhance their website's visibility, attract more organic traffic, and improve their chances of success in affiliate marketing. Regularly monitoring performance, staying updated on SEO trends and algorithm changes, and adapting strategies accordingly are also crucial for long-term SEO success.

# Paid Advertising Options

Paid advertising offers affiliate marketers the opportunity to reach a targeted audience quickly and efficiently.

**Some popular paid advertising options for affiliate marketers:**

**1. Google Ads (formerly Google AdWords):**
   - **Search Ads:** Bid on keywords related to your affiliate offers to appear at the top of Google search results, targeting users actively searching for relevant products or services.
   - **Display Ads:** Display visual ads on websites, blogs, and apps within the Google Display Network (GDN), targeting users based on demographics, interests, and browsing behavior.

- **Shopping Ads:** Promote affiliate products directly within Google Shopping results, showcasing product images, prices, and descriptions to users searching for specific products.

## 2. Social Media Advertising:

- **Facebook Ads:** Create targeted ad campaigns on Facebook and Instagram to reach users based on demographics, interests, behaviors, and connections, with options for various ad formats including image, video, carousel, and slideshow.

- **Twitter Ads:** Run Promoted Tweets, Promoted Accounts, or Promoted Trends campaigns on Twitter to reach a broader audience and promote affiliate offers to users interested in specific topics or hashtags.

- **LinkedIn Ads:** Target professionals and businesses with LinkedIn Ads, leveraging LinkedIn's extensive user data and professional targeting options to promote B2B affiliate offers or services.

## 3. Native Advertising:

- **Content Discovery Platforms:** Utilize native advertising platforms such as Outbrain, Taboola, or Revcontent to promote sponsored content or affiliate offers in the form of recommended articles, videos, or products on popular websites and media outlets.

- **Sponsored Content:** Partner with relevant publishers or media outlets to create sponsored content that seamlessly integrates your affiliate offers into editorial content, reaching engaged audiences in a non-disruptive manner.

4. Influencer Marketing:

- **Influencer Partnerships:** Collaborate with influencers, bloggers, vloggers, or social media personalities in your niche to promote your affiliate offers to their engaged audience through sponsored posts, videos, or endorsements.

- **Affiliate Influencers:** Recruit influencers as affiliates to promote your affiliate offers to their followers, earning commissions on sales generated through their unique affiliate links.

5. Programmatic Advertising:

- **Real-Time Bidding (RTB):** Utilize programmatic advertising platforms and exchanges to bid in real-time for ad impressions across a vast network of websites and apps, targeting specific audience segments based on demographics, interests, and behavior.

- **Retargeting:** Implement retargeting campaigns to re-engage users who have previously visited your website or interacted with your content, serving them personalized ads to encourage conversions and repeat visits.

## 6. Affiliate Networks and Platforms:

- **Affiliate Program Ads:** Promote your affiliate program to potential affiliates through advertising on affiliate networks and platforms such as Commission Junction, ShareASale, or ClickBank, attracting affiliates to join and promote your offers.

- **Affiliate Offers Promotion:** Advertise specific affiliate offers or products directly to consumers through affiliate networks' advertising options, reaching a broader audience of potential buyers.

## 7. Video Advertising:

- **YouTube Ads:** Run video ad campaigns on YouTube to reach users watching relevant videos or searching for related content, leveraging various ad formats such as TrueView, bumper ads, or sponsored cards to promote affiliate offers through video content.

- **In-Stream Ads:** Place video ads within streaming content on platforms like Hulu, Roku, or Amazon Prime Video to target users watching movies, TV shows, or live events, delivering your message to a captive audience.

**8. Email Marketing:**

- **Sponsored Emails:** Partner with email list owners, publishers, or media companies to sponsor dedicated email campaigns promoting your affiliate offers to their subscribers, leveraging their audience's trust and engagement to drive conversions.

Paid advertising offers affiliate marketers a range of options to promote affiliate offers, drive targeted traffic, and maximize conversions. By selecting the right advertising platforms, targeting options, and ad formats, affiliate marketers can effectively reach their desired audience and achieve their marketing goals. It's essential to track and analyze campaign performance, optimize ad creative and targeting, and stay updated on advertising trends and regulations to maximize ROI and long-term success.

## Utilizing Social Media for Traffic

Utilizing social media platforms effectively is an excellent strategy for driving traffic to your affiliate offers.

**The comprehensive guide on how to leverage social media for traffic generation:**

**1. Choose the Right Platforms:**
   - Identify social media platforms where your target audience is most active. Popular platforms for affiliate marketers include:
   - Facebook

- Instagram
- Twitter
- LinkedIn
- Pinterest
- YouTube
- TikTok

**2. Optimize Your Profiles:**

- Complete your profiles with relevant information, including a clear bio, profile picture, and website link.

- Use keywords related to your niche in your profile descriptions and usernames to enhance discoverability.

**3. Share Compelling Content:**

- Create valuable, engaging, and shareable content that resonates with your audience.

- Mix content formats such as images, videos, infographics, polls, and stories to keep your feed dynamic and engaging.

- Tailor your content to each platform's strengths and audience preferences.

**4. Build a Community:**

- Engage with your audience by responding to comments, messages, and mentions promptly.

- Foster conversations, ask questions, and encourage user-generated content to build a sense of community around your brand.

- Use hashtags strategically to increase visibility and reach new audiences.

**5. Promote Your Affiliate Offers:**

- Share your affiliate links strategically within your content, captions, and stories.

- Be transparent about your affiliate partnerships and disclose when you're promoting affiliate products.

- Offer value first before promoting products, ensuring your content provides solutions or addresses your audience's needs.

**6. Utilize Influencer Marketing:**

- Collaborate with influencers in your niche to reach their engaged audience and promote your affiliate offers.

- Partner with influencers for sponsored posts, reviews, giveaways, or takeovers to showcase your products or services.

**7. Run Paid Advertising Campaigns:**

- Leverage social media advertising options to reach a broader audience and drive targeted traffic to your affiliate offers.

- Utilize advanced targeting options based on demographics, interests, behaviors, and custom audiences to maximize ROI.

**8. Create Interactive Content:**

- Host live streams, Q&A sessions, polls, quizzes, or challenges to engage your audience and drive traffic to your affiliate links.

- Encourage participation and interaction to increase engagement and visibility on social media platforms.

**9. Cross-Promote Across Platforms:**

- Cross-promote your content and affiliate offers across multiple social media platforms to reach a wider audience and maximize exposure.

- Repurpose content for different platforms, optimizing formats and messaging to suit each platform's unique audience and features.

**10. Analyze and Optimize:**

- Monitor the performance of your social media efforts using analytics tools provided by each platform.

- Track key metrics such as reach, engagement, click-through rates (CTRs), and conversions to assess the effectiveness of your strategies.

- Experiment with different tactics, content formats, and posting schedules, and optimize your approach based on data insights.

Social media can be a powerful tool for driving traffic to your affiliate offers when used strategically. Choosing the right platforms, optimizing your profiles, sharing compelling content, building a community, promoting your affiliate offers authentically, utilizing influencer marketing, running paid advertising campaigns, creating interactive content, cross-promoting across platforms, and analyzing and optimizing your efforts, you can leverage social media to attract targeted traffic and maximize your affiliate marketing success.

## Building an Engaged Audience

Building an engaged audience is essential for the success of any affiliate marketing venture. An engaged audience not only increases the visibility of your affiliate offers but also fosters trust, loyalty, and ultimately, conversions.

**How you can effectively build and nurture an engaged audience:**

**1. Define Your Target Audience:**
   - **Demographics:** Identify the demographic characteristics of your target audience, such as age, gender, location, income level, and interests.
   - **Psychographics:** Understand the psychographic traits, values, attitudes, beliefs, and pain points of your audience to tailor your messaging and content effectively.

**2. Provide Value:**

- **Educational Content:** Share informative, valuable, and actionable content that addresses your audience's questions, challenges, and interests.

- **Entertaining Content:** Create engaging, entertaining, and shareable content that resonates with your audience's preferences and sense of humor.

- **Inspiring Content:** Motivate, inspire, and empower your audience with stories, examples, and insights that evoke emotions and encourage action.

**3. Be Authentic and Transparent:**

- **Authenticity:** Be genuine, authentic, and relatable in your interactions, content, and messaging to build trust and credibility with your audience.

- **Transparency:** Be transparent about your intentions, affiliations, and disclosures, especially when promoting affiliate products or sponsored content, to maintain integrity and trust.

**4. Engage and Interact:**

- **Two-Way Communication:** Foster meaningful interactions and conversations with your audience by responding to comments, messages, and mentions promptly.

- **Ask Questions:** Encourage engagement by asking questions, soliciting feedback, and inviting your audience to share their opinions, experiences, and ideas.

- **User-Generated Content:** Encourage user-generated content (UGC) such as testimonials, reviews, and user submissions to involve your audience in the content creation process and showcase their contributions.

**5. Build Community:**

- **Create Spaces for Interaction:** Establish online communities, forums, or groups where your audience can connect, share, and support each other.

- **Shared Values:** Foster a sense of belonging and community by aligning your brand with shared values, causes, or beliefs that resonate with your audience.

**6. Consistency and Frequency:**

- **Consistent Presence:** Maintain a consistent presence across your chosen platforms by posting regularly and engaging with your audience consistently.

- **Posting Schedule:** Establish a posting schedule or content calendar to ensure regular updates and maintain visibility in your audience's feeds.

**7. Offer Incentives and Rewards:**

- **Exclusive Content:** Provide exclusive content, sneak peeks, behind-the-scenes access, or early access to new products or offerings as incentives for your audience to engage and stay connected.

- **Contests and Giveaways:** Host contests, giveaways, or challenges to incentivize participation, reward engagement, and attract new followers.

**8. Listen and Adapt:**

- **Feedback Loop:** Listen to your audience's feedback, preferences, and concerns, and adapt your content, strategies, and offerings accordingly.

- **Monitor Trends:** Stay informed about industry trends, changes in audience behavior, and emerging platforms or technologies to stay relevant and adapt your approach.

**9. Collaborate and Partner:**

- **Collaborations:** Collaborate with influencers, brands, or organizations in your niche to leverage their audience, expertise, and resources to reach a wider audience and increase engagement.

- **Cross-Promotion:** Partner with complementary brands or creators to cross-promote each other's content, products, or services to mutual benefit.

**10. Measure and Improve:**

- **Analytics:** Use analytics tools to track key metrics such as engagement rates, reach, follower growth, and conversions to measure the effectiveness of your audience-building efforts.

- **Iterative Improvement:** Continuously analyze data insights, experiment with new tactics, and iterate on your strategies to optimize audience engagement and achieve your goals.

Building an engaged audience requires a combination of providing value, being authentic and transparent, engaging and interacting with your audience, fostering community, maintaining consistency, offering incentives and rewards, listening and adapting to feedback, collaborating and partnering with others, and measuring and improving your efforts over time. By focusing on building genuine relationships, delivering value, and nurturing trust, you can cultivate a loyal and engaged audience that supports your affiliate marketing endeavors and contributes to your long-term success.

# Chapter 6: Secrets to Maximizing Your Earnings

Maximizing earnings in affiliate marketing requires strategic planning, consistent effort, and a deep understanding of your audience and industry.

**Some secrets to help you optimize your affiliate marketing earnings:**

**1. Choose the Right Affiliate Programs:**
   - **High-Commission Programs:** Prioritize affiliate programs that offer competitive commissions and payout structures to maximize your earnings per sale or referral.
   - **Recurring Commissions:** Look for programs that offer recurring commissions for ongoing subscriptions or memberships, providing a steady stream of passive income over time.

**2. Focus on High-Converting Products:**

- **Product Research:** Identify products or services with high demand, relevance to your audience, and proven track records of conversion and customer satisfaction.

- **Conversion Optimization:** Optimize your promotional strategies and content to highlight the benefits, features, and value propositions of the products you're promoting, increasing conversion rates.

### 3. Build Trust and Authority:

- **Authenticity:** Build trust and credibility with your audience by promoting products and services you genuinely believe in and have personally tested or used.

- **Content Quality:** Create high-quality, informative, and valuable content that educates, entertains, or solves problems for your audience, positioning yourself as a trusted authority in your niche.

### 4. Diversify Your Revenue Streams:

- **Multiple Programs:** Join multiple affiliate programs across different niches or industries to diversify your income streams and mitigate risks associated with relying on a single source of revenue.

- **Monetization Methods:** Explore various monetization methods beyond affiliate marketing, such as display advertising, sponsored content, digital products, or online courses, to maximize your earnings potential.

**5. Optimize Your Traffic Sources:**

- **Targeted Traffic:** Focus on attracting targeted traffic to your affiliate offers by optimizing your SEO, content marketing, social media, email marketing, and paid advertising strategies.

- **Conversion Tracking:** Implement conversion tracking and analytics to identify which traffic sources and campaigns yield the highest conversion rates and ROI, allowing you to allocate resources effectively.

**6. Implement Upselling and Cross-Selling:**

- **Upselling:** Encourage customers to upgrade to higher-priced products or premium versions through upselling techniques such as bundle deals, product add-ons, or exclusive upgrades.

- **Cross-Selling:** Promote complementary products or related services to existing customers through cross-selling strategies, maximizing the value of each transaction and increasing your overall earnings.

**7. Leverage Seasonal Promotions and Trends:**

- **Seasonal Campaigns:** Capitalize on seasonal events, holidays, or trends by creating targeted promotions, discounts, or themed content around relevant products or services, driving increased sales and affiliate commissions.

- **Trend Analysis:** Stay updated on industry trends, consumer preferences, and emerging market opportunities to identify lucrative niches or products with high demand and profitability potential.

**8. Negotiate Higher Commissions:**

- **Negotiation Skills:** Develop negotiation skills and leverage your influence, audience size, and performance metrics to negotiate higher commission rates, exclusive deals, or custom partnerships with affiliate program managers or merchants.

- **Performance Incentives:** Offer to drive additional traffic, sales, or brand exposure in exchange for tiered commission structures, performance bonuses, or increased affiliate perks.

**9. Optimize for Mobile and Global Audiences:**

- **Mobile Optimization:** Ensure your website, content, and affiliate offers are optimized for mobile devices to accommodate the growing number of mobile users and capitalize on mobile-driven sales and conversions.

- **Global Reach:** Expand your reach and earnings potential by targeting international audiences, localizing content, and partnering with affiliate programs or networks that cater to global markets.

**10. Continuously Learn and Adapt:**

- **Stay Updated:** Stay informed about industry trends, affiliate marketing best practices, algorithm updates, and new technologies to adapt your strategies and stay ahead of the competition.

- **Experiment and Iterate:** Experiment with new tactics, test different strategies, and analyze performance metrics to identify what works best for your audience and niche, and iterate on your approach to maximize earnings over time.

Maximizing earnings in affiliate marketing requires a combination of selecting the right affiliate programs and products, building trust and authority with your audience, diversifying revenue streams, optimizing traffic sources, implementing upselling and cross-selling techniques, leveraging seasonal promotions and trends, negotiating higher commissions, optimizing for mobile and global audiences, and continuously learning and adapting to changes in the industry. By applying these secrets and refining your strategies based on performance insights, you can unlock your full earnings potential and achieve sustainable success in affiliate marketing.

# The Art of Persuasive Content

Crafting persuasive content is essential for driving engagement, building trust, and ultimately converting your audience into customers or clients.

**Here's how you can master the art of persuasive content creation:**

**1. Know Your Audience:**
 - Understand your audience's demographics, interests, pain points, and motivations.
 - Tailor your content to resonate with their needs and preferences.

**2. Start with a Compelling Hook:**
 - Grab your audience's attention from the start with a captivating headline, opening question, or intriguing statement.
 - Appeal to emotions, curiosity, or self-interest to pique curiosity and encourage further reading.

**3. Provide Value and Benefits:**
 - Clearly communicate the value proposition of your product or service.

- Highlight the benefits and solutions it offers to address your audience's problems or desires.

**4. Use Persuasive Language:**

- Employ persuasive language and power words to evoke emotions and influence action.
- Focus on benefits rather than features, emphasizing the positive outcomes your audience will experience.

**5. Build Credibility and Trust:**

- Establish credibility by showcasing your expertise, credentials, or social proof.
- Use testimonials, case studies, or endorsements to build trust and demonstrate the effectiveness of your offering.

**6. Create Engaging Content:**

- Tell stories, anecdotes, or use metaphors to make your content relatable and memorable.
- Incorporate multimedia elements such as images, videos, or infographics to enhance engagement and comprehension.

### 7. Address Objections:

- Anticipate and address potential objections or concerns your audience may have.

- Provide evidence, statistics, or testimonials to alleviate doubts and build confidence in your offering.

### 8. Use Social Proof:

- Showcase social proof such as customer reviews, ratings, or user-generated content to validate your claims and reinforce trust.

- Highlight endorsements from influencers, experts, or industry authorities to lend credibility to your content.

### 9. Create a Sense of Urgency:

- Encourage immediate action by creating a sense of urgency or scarcity.

- Use limited-time offers, exclusive deals, or countdown timers to motivate your audience to act quickly.

### 10. Call to Action (CTA):

- Clearly articulate the desired action you want your audience to take.

- Use persuasive CTAs that are specific, actionable, and aligned with your content's objectives.

**11. Test and Iterate:**

- Continuously test different messaging, formats, and strategies to optimize your content's persuasiveness.

- Analyze performance metrics and feedback to refine your approach and improve conversion rates over time.

**12. Be Authentic and Ethical:**

- Maintain authenticity and integrity in your content by being transparent and honest with your audience.

- Avoid manipulative tactics or deceptive practices that could damage your reputation and erode trust.

Mastering the art of persuasive content creation involves understanding your audience, crafting compelling messages, building credibility and trust, and motivating action through engaging storytelling, social proof, urgency, and effective CTAs. By following these principles and continuously refining your approach based on feedback and data insights, you can create content that resonates with your audience, drives engagement, and achieves your desired outcomes.

## Building Trust with Your Audience

Building trust with your audience is essential for long-term success in affiliate marketing. Trust forms the foundation of strong relationships, encourages engagement, and ultimately leads to higher conversions.

**These can help you on how you can build trust with your audience:**

**1. Be Authentic and Transparent:**

- Be genuine, honest, and transparent in your interactions, messaging, and promotions.

- Disclose your affiliations, sponsorships, and any potential conflicts of interest to maintain integrity and credibility.

## 2. Provide Value:

- Offer valuable, informative, and relevant content that addresses your audience's needs, challenges, and interests.

- Focus on helping and educating your audience rather than solely promoting products or services.

## 3. Consistency:

- Maintain a consistent presence across your chosen platforms by posting regularly and engaging with your audience consistently.

- Deliver on your promises and commitments to establish reliability and dependability.

## 4. Build Authority:

- Demonstrate expertise, knowledge, and credibility in your niche through your content, experiences, and achievements.

- Share valuable insights, tips, and advice that showcase your expertise and position you as a trusted authority.

**5. Engage and Interact:**
   - Foster meaningful interactions and conversations with your audience by responding to comments, messages, and mentions promptly.
   - Encourage feedback, questions, and discussions to create a sense of community and involvement.

**6. Use Social Proof:**
   - Showcase social proof such as testimonials, reviews, ratings, and user-generated content to validate your claims and build credibility.
   - Highlight endorsements from satisfied customers, influencers, or industry experts to reinforce trust.

**7. Be Customer-Centric:**
   - Prioritize the needs and interests of your audience above your own agenda or objectives.

- Listen to feedback, address concerns, and adapt your strategies based on audience preferences and feedback.

## 8. Deliver Quality:

- Ensure the products or services you promote are of high quality, reliable, and aligned with your audience's expectations.

- Recommend products or services that you genuinely believe in and have personally tested or used.

## 9. Build Relationships:

- Invest time and effort in building genuine relationships with your audience based on trust, respect, and mutual understanding.

- Personalize your interactions, acknowledge individual preferences, and show appreciation for your audience's support.

## 10. Be Accessible:

- Make yourself accessible and approachable to your audience through various channels such as email, social media, or community forums.

- Encourage open communication and feedback, and be responsive to inquiries and messages.

**11. Share Your Story:**
- Share your personal story, experiences, and journey to connect with your audience on a deeper level.
- Be authentic and vulnerable in sharing both successes and challenges to humanize your brand and foster relatability.

**12. Uphold Ethical Standards:**
- Operate with integrity and uphold ethical standards in all your interactions and business practices.
- Avoid engaging in deceptive or manipulative tactics that could undermine trust and damage your reputation.

Building trust with your audience is a gradual process that requires authenticity, consistency, value, engagement, and integrity. By prioritizing transparency, providing value, engaging authentically, leveraging social proof, and focusing on building genuine relationships, you can establish trust with your audience and cultivate a loyal and supportive community that drives success in affiliate marketing.

## High-Conversion Techniques

Achieving high conversion rates is the ultimate goal for affiliate marketers. Implementing effective high-conversion techniques can significantly boost your affiliate marketing success.

**Some strategies to help you optimize your conversion rates:**

**1. Understand Your Audience:**
   - Conduct thorough audience research to understand their demographics, preferences, pain points, and purchasing behavior.
   - Tailor your messaging, content, and offers to resonate with your audience's needs and motivations.

**2. Create Compelling Content:**

- Craft attention-grabbing headlines, compelling copy, and persuasive calls to action (CTAs) that prompt immediate action.

- Use storytelling, emotional appeals, and persuasive language to engage your audience and drive them towards conversion.

**3. Focus on Benefits, Not Features:**

- Emphasize the benefits and outcomes of the products or services you're promoting rather than just listing their features.

- Clearly communicate how your affiliate offers solve your audience's problems or fulfill their desires to compel action.

**4. Use Visuals Effectively:**

- Incorporate high-quality images, videos, infographics, and multimedia elements to enhance the visual appeal of your content.

- Visuals can help convey information more effectively and capture your audience's attention, leading to higher engagement and conversions.

**5. Leverage Social Proof:**

- Showcase testimonials, reviews, ratings, case studies, and user-generated content to build credibility and trust with your audience.

- Highlight success stories and endorsements from satisfied customers or influencers to validate your affiliate offers.

**6. Offer Incentives and Bonuses:**

- Provide exclusive discounts, promotions, bonuses, or limited-time offers to incentivize immediate action and drive conversions.

- Create a sense of urgency or scarcity to encourage your audience to take advantage of the offer before it expires.

**7. Optimize Landing Pages:**

- Design clean, visually appealing, and user-friendly landing pages that are optimized for conversions.

- Include clear and compelling CTAs, concise copy, relevant images, and trust signals to guide visitors towards conversion.

**8. Implement A/B Testing:**

- Conduct A/B tests on various elements of your campaigns, such as headlines, CTAs, visuals, and offer structures, to identify what resonates best with your audience.

- Use data-driven insights to refine your strategies and optimize conversion rates over time.

**9. Streamline the Checkout Process:**

- Simplify the checkout process for your audience by minimizing friction, reducing form fields, and offering multiple payment options.

- Remove distractions and unnecessary steps to streamline the conversion path and increase completion rates.

**10. Retarget Interested Visitors:**

- Implement retargeting campaigns to re-engage visitors who have shown interest in your affiliate offers but haven't completed the desired action.

- Serve personalized ads or reminders to remind them of the benefits of your offer and encourage them to convert.

**11. Provide Exceptional Customer Support:**

- Offer responsive and helpful customer support to address any pre-purchase inquiries, concerns, or objections.

- Provide reassurance and assistance to potential customers to overcome hesitations and instill confidence in their decision to convert.

**12. Track and Analyze Performance:**

- Use tracking tools and analytics to monitor the performance of your campaigns, track conversion metrics, and identify areas for improvement.

- Analyze conversion funnels, attribution models, and user behavior to optimize your strategies and maximize conversion rates.

By implementing these high-conversion techniques, you can optimize your affiliate marketing efforts and drive higher conversion rates. Understanding your audience, creating compelling content, leveraging social proof, optimizing landing pages, and continuously testing and refining your strategies, you can increase conversions and achieve your affiliate marketing goals.

# Tracking and Analyzing Performance

Tracking and analyzing performance is crucial for optimizing your affiliate marketing efforts and maximizing your return on investment (ROI).

**How you can effectively track and analyze the performance of your affiliate campaigns:**

**1. Set Clear Goals:**
   - Define specific, measurable, and actionable goals for your affiliate marketing campaigns, such as sales, leads, clicks, or revenue targets.
   - Align your goals with your overall business objectives and key performance indicators (KPIs) to measure success effectively.

**2. Use Tracking Tools:**
   - Implement reliable tracking tools and technologies to monitor the performance of your affiliate campaigns accurately.
   - Utilize affiliate tracking software provided by affiliate networks or platforms, or integrate third-

party tracking solutions such as Google Analytics, ClickMeter, or Voluum.

**3. Track Key Metrics:**

- Monitor key performance metrics such as clicks, conversions, conversion rates, sales, revenue, average order value (AOV), and return on investment (ROI).

- Segment and analyze data based on different parameters such as traffic sources, demographics, devices, and geographical locations to gain insights into campaign performance.

**4. Set Up Conversion Tracking:**

- Implement conversion tracking pixels or codes on your website or landing pages to track affiliate conversions accurately.

- Ensure proper tracking of affiliate referrals, sales, and actions to attribute conversions back to the appropriate affiliate campaigns or sources.

**5. Analyze Conversion Funnels:**

- Map out the conversion funnel for your affiliate campaigns to understand the journey users take from initial engagement to conversion.

- Identify potential bottlenecks, drop-off points, or areas of friction within the funnel and optimize them to improve conversion rates.

**6. Monitor Traffic Sources:**

- Analyze the performance of different traffic sources and channels driving traffic to your affiliate offers, such as organic search, paid advertising, social media, email marketing, or referral traffic.

- Identify top-performing traffic sources and allocate resources accordingly to maximize ROI and conversions.

**7. Segment Audiences:**

- Segment your audience based on various criteria such as demographics, interests, behaviors, or engagement levels.

- Analyze the performance of different audience segments to tailor your messaging, offers, and targeting strategies effectively.

**8. Test and Experiment:**

- Conduct A/B tests or split tests on various elements of your affiliate campaigns, such as ad creatives, headlines, landing page designs, or offers.

- Experiment with different strategies, tactics, and variables to identify what resonates best with your audience and drives the highest conversions.

**9. Analyze ROI and Profitability:**

- Calculate the return on investment (ROI) and profitability of your affiliate campaigns by comparing the costs incurred (e.g., advertising spend, affiliate commissions) with the revenue generated.

- Evaluate the effectiveness of your campaigns in terms of revenue generated per dollar spent and adjust your strategies accordingly to optimize ROI.

**10. Monitor Trends and Insights:**

- Stay updated on industry trends, consumer behavior, and market insights relevant to your niche and affiliate offers.

- Analyze data trends, patterns, and performance insights to identify opportunities, capitalize on emerging trends, and stay ahead of the competition.

**11. Regularly Review Performance:**
- Schedule regular reviews and performance audits of your affiliate campaigns to assess progress towards your goals and identify areas for improvement.
- Use performance reports, dashboards, and analytics tools to track performance over time and make data-driven decisions.

**12. Iterate and Optimize:**
- Continuously iterate on your affiliate marketing strategies based on performance insights, test results, and feedback.
- Optimize campaigns, refine targeting, adjust messaging, and reallocate resources to improve performance, maximize conversions, and achieve your goals.

Tracking and analyzing performance is essential for optimizing your affiliate marketing campaigns, identifying opportunities for improvement, and maximizing your ROI. By setting clear goals, using tracking tools, monitoring key metrics, analyzing conversion funnels, segmenting audiences, testing and experimenting, analyzing ROI, staying informed about trends, regularly reviewing performance, and iterating and optimizing strategies, you can drive better results and achieve success in affiliate marketing.

# Appendix

In the appendix, you'll find additional resources, tools, and information to further enhance your understanding and proficiency in affiliate marketing. These supplementary materials are designed to complement the knowledge and strategies outlined in the main guide and provide valuable insights and support for your affiliate marketing endeavors.

**Here's what you can expect to find in the appendix:**

**1. Recommended Reading:**
   - A curated list of books, blogs, articles, and other educational resources on affiliate marketing, digital marketing, and related topics.
   - Explore in-depth guides, case studies, and expert insights to deepen your knowledge and stay updated on industry trends and best practices.

**2. Glossary of Terms:**

- A comprehensive glossary of key terms, acronyms, and definitions commonly used in affiliate marketing and digital advertising.

- Enhance your understanding of industry-specific terminology and concepts to navigate affiliate marketing discussions and resources with confidence.

**3. Tools and Software:**

- An overview of essential tools, software, and platforms to streamline your affiliate marketing operations, track performance, and optimize your campaigns.

- Discover affiliate networks, tracking solutions, content creation tools, keyword research platforms, and more to enhance your productivity and efficiency.

**4. Legal and Compliance Resources:**

- Guidance on legal and compliance considerations for affiliate marketers, including disclosure requirements, privacy regulations, and best practices for maintaining compliance.

- Ensure that your affiliate marketing activities adhere to relevant laws, regulations, and industry standards to mitigate risks and protect your brand reputation.

**5. Case Studies and Success Stories:**
- Inspiring case studies and success stories from affiliate marketers who have achieved notable results and overcome challenges in their affiliate marketing journeys.
- Learn from real-world examples, strategies, and insights to inform your own affiliate marketing strategies and tactics.

**6. Frequently Asked Questions (FAQs):**
- Answers to commonly asked questions about affiliate marketing, affiliate programs, tracking, payments, compliance, and other relevant topics.
- Find solutions to common challenges, clarify misconceptions, and gain valuable insights into the affiliate marketing ecosystem.

**7. Additional Resources:**

- Links to relevant industry associations, forums, podcasts, webinars, and events for affiliate marketers to further expand their knowledge, network with peers, and stay connected with the affiliate marketing community.

- Access additional resources and support to fuel your growth and success in the dynamic and evolving field of affiliate marketing.

The appendix serves as a valuable reference and supplementary resource to support your affiliate marketing journey. Whether you're looking to deepen your knowledge, streamline your operations, or stay informed about industry developments, the appendix provides the tools and information you need to thrive in the affiliate marketing landscape.

# Glossary of Affiliate Marketing Terms

**A/B Testing:**

A method of comparing two versions of a webpage, ad, or other marketing asset to determine which one performs better.

**Affiliate:**
A person or entity that promotes products or services of another company (the merchant) in exchange for a commission on sales or leads generated through their referrals.

**Affiliate Agreement:**
A contract or agreement between an affiliate and a merchant outlining the terms and conditions of their partnership, including commission rates, payment terms, and promotional guidelines.

**Affiliate Manager:**
A person responsible for managing an affiliate program, recruiting affiliates, providing support, and optimizing performance to maximize affiliate revenue.

**Affiliate Network:**

An intermediary platform that connects affiliates with merchants, facilitating affiliate marketing partnerships and tracking affiliate referrals, sales, and commissions.

**Conversion:**
The completion of a desired action by a user, such as making a purchase, filling out a form, subscribing to a newsletter, or downloading an app.

**Conversion Rate:**
The percentage of visitors who complete a desired action, such as making a purchase or signing up, out of the total number of visitors to a website or landing page.

**Cookie:**
A small piece of data stored on a user's device by a website, used to track user interactions, preferences, and affiliate referrals over time.

**Cost Per Action (CPA):**
An affiliate marketing pricing model where advertisers pay affiliates a commission for each

specified action completed by a referred user, such as a sale, lead, or form submission.

**Cost Per Click (CPC):**
An affiliate marketing pricing model where advertisers pay affiliates a commission for each click on their affiliate links, regardless of whether a conversion occurs.

**Cost Per Lead (CPL):**
An affiliate marketing pricing model where advertisers pay affiliates a commission for each qualified lead generated through their referrals, typically based on user sign-ups or form submissions.

**Cost Per Sale (CPS):**
An affiliate marketing pricing model where advertisers pay affiliates a commission for each sale generated through their referrals, usually based on a percentage of the sale amount or a fixed dollar amount.

**EPC (Earnings Per Click):**

The average amount of earnings generated by an affiliate per click on their affiliate links, calculated by dividing total earnings by total clicks.

**Landing Page:**
A standalone web page designed specifically for a marketing campaign or promotion, with the primary goal of encouraging visitors to take a specific action, such as making a purchase or signing up.

**Merchant:**
A company or business that sells products or services and participates in an affiliate marketing program by paying commissions to affiliates for driving sales or leads.

**Pay Per Click (PPC):**
An advertising model where advertisers pay a fee each time their ad is clicked, commonly used in search engine advertising (e.g., Google Ads) and affiliate marketing campaigns.

**Revenue Share:**

An affiliate marketing commission structure where affiliates earn a percentage of the revenue generated by sales or transactions they refer to a merchant.

**Subaffiliate:**
An affiliate referred to an affiliate program by another affiliate, typically earning a portion of the commissions generated by their referrals.

**Tracking:**
The process of monitoring and recording user interactions, conversions, and affiliate referrals through tracking codes, cookies, or other tracking mechanisms.

**White Label:**
A product or service that is rebranded and resold by affiliates under their own brand name, often with customizable features or branding options.

This glossary provides a comprehensive overview of key terms and concepts in affiliate marketing, helping you navigate the affiliate marketing ecosystem and understand industry-specific terminology. Whether you're new to affiliate marketing or a seasoned professional, this glossary serves as a valuable reference for enhancing your knowledge and proficiency in the field.

# Recommended Tools and Resources

**1. Affiliate Networks:**

  - **ShareASale:** A leading affiliate marketing network with a wide range of merchants and products across various niches.

  - **CJ Affiliate (formerly Commission Junction):** A global affiliate marketing network with a diverse selection of advertisers and advanced tracking and reporting capabilities.

  - **Rakuten Advertising (formerly Rakuten Marketing):** An affiliate network offering access to top brands and comprehensive tracking and reporting tools.

### 2. Tracking and Analytics:

- **Google Analytics:** A powerful web analytics platform for tracking website traffic, user behavior, and conversions.

- Voluum: A comprehensive affiliate tracking and analytics platform with advanced features for campaign optimization and performance monitoring.

- ClickMeter: A URL tracking and link management platform that enables affiliates to track clicks, conversions, and campaign performance.

**3. Keyword Research and SEO:**

- SEMrush: A versatile SEO tool for keyword research, competitive analysis, backlink analysis, and site auditing.

- Ahrefs: A comprehensive SEO toolkit with features for keyword research, rank tracking, content analysis, and link building.

- KeywordTool.io: A keyword research tool that provides keyword suggestions and search volume data from Google, YouTube, Bing, and other platforms.

**4. Content Creation and Management:**

- **WordPress:** A popular content management system (CMS) for creating and managing websites, blogs, and online stores.

- **Canva:** A user-friendly graphic design tool for creating stunning visuals, social media graphics, and promotional materials.

- **Grammarly:** A writing assistant tool that helps improve grammar, punctuation, and readability in your content.

**5. Email Marketing:**

- **Mailchimp:** An email marketing platform with features for designing, sending, and tracking email campaigns, as well as building subscriber lists.

- **ConvertKit:** An email marketing automation platform designed for bloggers, content creators, and online entrepreneurs.

- **AWeber:** An email marketing tool with features for creating email newsletters, automating campaigns, and segmenting subscribers.

**6. Social Media Management:**

- **Hootsuite:** A social media management platform for scheduling posts, monitoring conversations, and analyzing performance across multiple social networks.

- **Buffer:** A social media scheduling tool that allows you to plan, publish, and analyze posts on various social media platforms.

- **Sprout Social:** A comprehensive social media management and analytics platform with features for engagement, publishing, and reporting.

## 7. Website Optimization and Conversion Rate Optimization (CRO):

- **OptinMonster:** A conversion optimization tool for creating and deploying lead capture forms, pop-ups, and other conversion-focused campaigns.

- **Unbounce:** A landing page builder that enables you to create and optimize custom landing pages for your affiliate marketing campaigns.

- **Hotjar:** A behavior analytics tool that provides insights into user behavior through heatmaps, session recordings, and surveys.

## 8. Legal and Compliance:

- **TermsFeed:** A platform for generating custom privacy policies, terms of service, and other legal documents for your website or online business.

- **iubenda:*m** A privacy and cookie policy generator that helps you comply with global privacy regulations such as GDPR and CCPA.

- **FTC Affiliate Disclosure Guidelines:** Resources and guidelines from the Federal Trade Commission (FTC) on disclosing affiliate relationships and endorsements.

**9. Learning and Education:**

- **Affiliate Marketing Forums:** Join affiliate marketing forums and communities such as Warrior Forum, Affilorama, and STM Forum to network with other affiliates, share insights, and learn from industry experts.

- **Affiliate Marketing Blogs:** Follow popular affiliate marketing blogs such as Affiliate Summit, Affiliate Insider, and Charles Ngo's Blog for tips, strategies, and industry news.

- **Affiliate Marketing Courses:** Enroll in affiliate marketing courses and training programs offered by platforms like Udemy, Coursera, and Skillshare to deepen your knowledge and skills.

These recommended tools and resources cover a wide range of areas essential for affiliate marketing success, including affiliate networks, tracking and analytics, keyword research and SEO, content creation, email marketing, social media management, website optimization, legal compliance, and learning and education. Whether you're just starting or looking to scale your affiliate marketing efforts, these tools and resources can help you streamline your operations, optimize your campaigns, and achieve your affiliate marketing goals.

## Sample Email Templates

**Here are some sample email templates you can use for various affiliate marketing purposes:**

**1. Affiliate Partnership Inquiry:**
**Subject:** Inquiry Regarding Affiliate Partnership Opportunity

Hi [Merchant's Name],

I hope this email finds you well. My name is [Your Name], and I am a [Your Niche] blogger/content creator with a growing audience interested in [relevant topic or niche].

I am reaching out to express my interest in potentially partnering with your company as an affiliate. I am impressed by your products/services, and I believe they would resonate well with my audience. I am confident that I can effectively promote your offerings and drive valuable traffic and conversions.

I would appreciate the opportunity to discuss the possibility of establishing an affiliate partnership further. Please let me know if you would be open to exploring this opportunity further, and if so, I would be happy to provide more information about my audience, reach, and promotional strategies.

Thank you for considering my proposal. I look forward to the possibility of collaborating with you.

Best regards,
[Your Name]
[Your Contact Information]

**2. Affiliate Promotion Announcement:**
**Subject:** Exciting News: Exclusive Offer Inside!

Hi [Subscriber's Name],

I hope you're doing well! I'm excited to share some great news with you. As an affiliate partner of [Merchant's Name], I've secured an exclusive offer just for you!

For a limited time only, you can [describe the offer, such as a discount, free trial, or special promotion]. This is a fantastic opportunity to [highlight the benefits of the offer and why it's valuable to the recipient].

To take advantage of this special offer, simply [include instructions on how to redeem the offer, such as using a unique promo code or clicking on an affiliate link].

Don't miss out on this opportunity to [mention the urgency or scarcity of the offer, if applicable]. Act fast and [call to action encouraging recipients to take advantage of the offer].

If you have any questions or need assistance, feel free to reach out to me directly. Thank you for your continued support!

Best regards,
[Your Name]
[Your Contact Information]

**3. Follow-Up Reminder:**
**Subject:** Friendly Reminder: Exclusive Offer Expires Soon!

Hi [Subscriber's Name],

I hope you're doing well! I wanted to send you a quick reminder about the exclusive offer I mentioned in my previous email.

Just a friendly heads up that the [offer details] will be expiring soon, so be sure to take advantage of it before it's too late!

Don't miss out on this fantastic opportunity to [reiterate the benefits of the offer]. Simply [include instructions on how to redeem the offer].

If you have any questions or need assistance, don't hesitate to reach out to me. I'm here to help!

Best regards,
[Your Name]
[Your Contact Information]

These sample email templates can be customized and adapted to suit your specific affiliate marketing needs, whether you're reaching out to potential partners, promoting affiliate offers to your audience, or sending follow-up reminders. Personalize the templates with your own branding, messaging, and contact information to create effective and engaging email communications.

# Additional Reading and References

Here are some additional reading recommendations and references to further enhance your knowledge and understanding of affiliate marketing:

**Books:**
1. **"Affiliate Marketing:** Secrets" by K. M. Timur
2. **"Affiliate Marketing:** Proven Step By Step Guide To Make Passive Income" by Kevin Ulaner
3. **"Affiliate Marketing:** How to Become a Seven Figure Affiliate Marketer in Today's Digital World" by Kasim K. Malik
4. **"Affiliate Marketing:** How to Make Money Online and Build Your Own $100,000+ Affiliate Marketing Online Business" by Anthony Parker

**Blogs and Websites:**

1. [Affiliate Summit](https://www.affiliatesummit.com/) - Industry news, insights, and resources for affiliate marketers.

2. [Affiliate Insider](https://affiliateinsider.com/) - Affiliate marketing news, interviews, and expert advice.

3. [Charles Ngo's Blog](https://charlesngo.com/) - Affiliate marketing tips, case studies, and strategies from industry expert Charles Ngo.

4. [Pat Flynn's Smart Passive Income Blog](https://www.smartpassiveincome.com/blog/) - Insights and strategies for building passive income streams, including affiliate marketing.

**Online Courses and Training:**

1. [Affiliate Marketing Mastery by Stefan James](https://www.affiliatemarketingmastery.com/) - Comprehensive course on affiliate marketing strategies, tactics, and implementation.

2. [Commission Hero by Robby Blanchard](https://www.commissionhero.com/) -

Training program focused on affiliate marketing with Facebook ads.

3. [Affiliate Marketing for Beginners by Udemy](https://www.udemy.com/course/affiliate-marketing-for-beginners-course/) - Beginner-friendly course covering the fundamentals of affiliate marketing.

4. [The Authority Site System by Authority Hacker](https://www.authorityhacker.com/tass/) - Course on building authority affiliate websites and scaling affiliate marketing businesses.

**Industry Associations and Events:**

1. [Affiliate Summit](https://www.affiliatesummit.com/) - Leading affiliate marketing conference and networking event.

2. [Performance Marketing Association (PMA)](https://thepma.org/) - Trade association representing the performance marketing industry.

3. [Affiliate Marketing Meetups](https://www.meetup.com/topics/affiliate-marketing/) - Local and virtual meetups for affiliate marketers to network and share insights.

4. [Affiliate World Conferences](https://www.affiliateworldconferences.com/) - Global events for affiliate marketers featuring industry experts, networking opportunities, and educational sessions.

**Podcasts:**

1. [The Affiliate Guy Podcast](https://www.affiliateguy.com/podcast/) - Podcast hosted by affiliate marketing expert Matt McWilliams featuring tips, strategies, and interviews.

2. [The Smart Passive Income Podcast](https://www.smartpassiveincome.com/shows/spi/) - Podcast hosted by Pat Flynn covering various topics related to online business, including affiliate marketing.

3. [The Authority Hacker Podcast](https://www.authorityhacker.com/podcast/) - Podcast hosted by Gael Breton and Mark Webster covering affiliate marketing, SEO, and authority site building.

4. [The Affiliate Journey Podcast](https://www.theaffiliatejourneypodcast.co

m/) - Podcast featuring interviews with successful affiliate marketers sharing their journey, strategies, and insights.

These additional reading recommendations and references cover a wide range of topics and resources to help you deepen your understanding, refine your strategies, and stay updated on the latest trends and developments in affiliate marketing. Whether you prefer books, blogs, online courses, industry events, podcasts, or associations, there are plenty of opportunities to expand your knowledge and skills in affiliate marketing.

# Conclusion

Effective affiliate marketing requires a combination of strategic planning, thoughtful execution, and continuous optimization. Throughout this guide, we've explored various aspects of affiliate marketing, from understanding the fundamentals to implementing advanced strategies for success.

Affiliate marketing presents a tremendous opportunity for individuals and businesses to generate passive income, expand their reach, and monetize their online presence. By partnering with reputable affiliate programs, selecting high-converting products or services, and leveraging persuasive content and marketing techniques, you can attract and engage your target audience while driving conversions and earning commissions.

Building trust and credibility with your audience is paramount in affiliate marketing. By providing value, being transparent, and delivering exceptional customer experiences, you can foster long-lasting relationships that lead to loyalty and repeat business. Additionally, tracking and analyzing performance metrics allows you to measure the effectiveness of your efforts, identify areas for improvement, and optimize your strategies for maximum results.

As you kick start on your affiliate marketing journey, remember to stay informed about industry trends, adapt to changes in consumer behavior, and continuously refine your approach based on data-driven insights. With dedication, perseverance, and a commitment to delivering value, you can achieve success and unlock the full potential of affiliate marketing as a sustainable source of income.

Whether you're just starting or looking to scale your affiliate marketing efforts, remember that success doesn't happen overnight. It requires patience, experimentation, and a willingness to learn from both successes and setbacks. By staying focused on your goals, maintaining integrity in your actions, and prioritizing the needs of your audience, you can build a thriving affiliate marketing business that stands the test of time.

Thank you for embarking on this affiliate marketing journey with us. Here's to your success in the exciting world of affiliate marketing!

## Recap of Key Points

**1. Understanding Affiliate Marketing:**
- Affiliate marketing is a performance-based marketing strategy where affiliates earn commissions for promoting products or services and driving sales or leads through their referrals.

**2. Getting Started:**
- Choose a niche that aligns with your interests, expertise, and target audience.
- Research and select affiliate programs and products relevant to your niche.
- Build a platform (e.g., website, blog, social media) to attract and engage your audience.

**3. Choosing the Right Niche:**

- Consider factors such as market demand, competition, profitability, and personal interests when selecting a niche.
- Aim for a balance between niche specificity and audience size to maximize your potential reach and impact.

### 4. Finding and Joining Affiliate Programs:
- Research and evaluate affiliate programs based on factors such as commission rates, product quality, tracking capabilities, and payment terms.
- Join multiple affiliate programs to diversify your revenue streams and maximize earning potential.

### 5. Building Your Platform:
- Create a professional and user-friendly website or blog to serve as your affiliate marketing hub.
- Optimize your platform for search engines (SEO), user experience (UX), and mobile responsiveness.
- Leverage content marketing, social media, email marketing, and other channels to drive traffic and engage your audience.

### 6. Content Creation and Promotion:

- Produce high-quality, valuable content that educates, entertains, or solves problems for your audience.
- Incorporate affiliate links naturally within your content, focusing on relevance and context.
- Promote your affiliate offers through various channels, including blog posts, videos, social media posts, email newsletters, and webinars.

## 7. Traffic Generation and Conversion Optimization:

- Implement strategies to attract targeted traffic to your platform, such as SEO, social media marketing, paid advertising, and influencer partnerships.
- Optimize your conversion funnel, landing pages, and calls to action (CTAs) to maximize conversions and revenue.
- Track and analyze key performance metrics to measure the effectiveness of your affiliate marketing efforts and make data-driven decisions.

## 8. Building Relationships and Trust:

- Prioritize building authentic relationships with your audience based on trust, transparency, and value.
- Provide genuine recommendations, honest reviews, and helpful insights to establish credibility and foster loyalty.
- Disclose your affiliate relationships openly and ethically to maintain trust and integrity with your audience.

Affiliate marketing offers a lucrative opportunity to generate passive income online by promoting products or services you believe in to a targeted audience. By understanding the fundamentals, selecting the right niche, joining reputable affiliate programs, building a strong platform, creating valuable content, driving targeted traffic, optimizing conversions, and building trust with your audience, you can succeed as an affiliate marketer and achieve your financial and lifestyle goals.

# Developing a Long-Term Strategy

Developing a long-term strategy is crucial for sustained success in affiliate marketing.

**How to create a strategic plan that sets you up for long-term growth and profitability:**

**1. Define Your Goals:**
- Clarify your long-term objectives, whether it's to achieve a certain level of passive income, build a sustainable online business, or establish yourself as an authority in your niche.
- Break down your goals into specific, measurable, achievable, relevant, and time-bound (SMART) targets to track your progress effectively.

**2. Choose Your Niche Wisely:**
- Select a niche that aligns with your interests, expertise, and passions, but also has significant market demand and growth potential.

- Conduct thorough research to identify profitable niches, analyze competition, and understand the needs and preferences of your target audience.

### 3. Build a Strong Foundation:
- Invest time and effort in creating a professional and user-friendly website or blog that serves as the central hub for your affiliate marketing activities.
- Focus on providing valuable content, optimizing for search engines, and cultivating a loyal audience base through engagement and interaction.

### 4. Diversify Your Revenue Streams:
- Don't rely solely on one affiliate program or revenue source. Diversify your income streams by joining multiple affiliate programs, exploring different niches, and experimenting with various monetization methods.
- Incorporate other revenue streams such as display advertising, sponsored content, digital products, or consulting services to supplement your affiliate earnings.

### 5. Build Relationships and Partnerships:

- Create meaningful relationships with your audience, fellow affiliates, influencers, and industry experts. Networking and collaboration can open doors to new opportunities and expand your reach.

- Collaborate with merchants and brands on exclusive promotions, sponsored content, or co-branded campaigns to create mutually beneficial partnerships.

**6. Focus on Quality Over Quantity:**

- Prioritize quality over quantity when creating content, promoting products, and engaging with your audience. Delivering value and building trust should be your primary focus.

- Avoid spammy tactics, aggressive promotion, or sacrificing integrity for short-term gains. Authenticity and credibility are essential for long-term success.

**7. Invest in Continuous Learning and Improvement:**

- Stay updated on industry trends, emerging technologies, and best practices through ongoing education, training, and professional development.

- Test new strategies, track performance metrics, analyze results, and iterate based on data-driven insights to optimize your efforts and stay ahead of the curve.

**8. Stay Committed and Persistent:**
- Rome wasn't built in a day, and neither is a successful affiliate marketing business. Stay committed to your goals, stay persistent in your efforts, and be prepared to weather challenges and setbacks along the way.
- Celebrate your successes, learn from your failures, and keep pushing forward with resilience, determination, and a growth mindset.

Following these steps and developing a long-term strategy focused on building a strong foundation, diversifying revenue streams, cultivating relationships, delivering value, and embracing continuous improvement, you can position yourself for sustainable success and longevity in the competitive world of affiliate marketing. Keep your eyes on the prize, stay adaptable to changes in the industry, and remember that consistency and perseverance are key to achieving your long-term goals.

## Staying Updated with Industry Trends

Staying updated with industry trends is essential for staying competitive and relevant in affiliate marketing.

**How to stay informed about the latest developments and trends in the industry:**

**1. Follow Industry Blogs and Websites:**
- Subscribe to reputable affiliate marketing blogs, news websites, and industry publications for regular updates, insights, and analysis.
- Some popular blogs and websites include Affiliate Summit, Affiliate Insider, Affiliate Marketing Forum, and PerformanceIN.

**2. Join Online Communities and Forums:**

- Participate in affiliate marketing forums, discussion groups, and online communities to connect with fellow affiliates, share experiences, and exchange insights.
- Platforms like Warrior Forum, Affilorama, STM Forum, and Reddit's affiliate marketing subreddits are great places to engage with other industry professionals.

**3. Attend Industry Events and Conferences:**
- Attend affiliate marketing conferences, summits, and workshops to network with industry experts, learn from keynote speakers, and stay updated on the latest trends.
- Events like Affiliate Summit, Affiliate World Conferences, and industry-specific meetups offer valuable opportunities for learning and networking.

**4. Follow Influential Figures and Thought Leaders:**
- Follow influential figures and thought leaders in the affiliate marketing industry on social media platforms like Twitter, LinkedIn, and Instagram.

- Engage with their content, participate in discussions, and stay informed about their perspectives, insights, and recommendations.

**5. Join Webinars and Podcasts:**
- Tune in to affiliate marketing webinars, podcasts, and online workshops hosted by industry experts and thought leaders.
- Platforms like Affiliate Summit, Smart Passive Income, and Authority Hacker offer valuable resources and insights through their webinars and podcasts.

**6. Monitor Industry News and Updates:**
- Keep an eye on industry news, announcements, and updates from affiliate networks, merchants, and regulatory bodies.
- Set up Google Alerts or use RSS feeds to monitor relevant keywords, topics, and industry developments.

**7. Experiment and Test New Strategies:**

- Stay proactive and open-minded by experimenting with new strategies, tools, and technologies in your affiliate marketing campaigns.
- Test different tactics, analyze results, and iterate based on data-driven insights to stay ahead of the curve.

**8. Continuously Educate Yourself:**
- Invest in ongoing education, training, and professional development to stay updated on the latest trends and best practices.
- Enroll in affiliate marketing courses, attend workshops, and read books authored by industry experts to deepen your knowledge and skills.

By actively engaging with industry blogs, online communities, events, influencers, webinars, podcasts, news updates, and educational resources, you can stay informed about the latest trends, developments, and opportunities in the dynamic and ever-evolving field of affiliate marketing. Embrace a lifelong learning mindset, stay adaptable to changes, and leverage new insights and strategies to drive success in your affiliate marketing endeavors.

# Final Words of Encouragement

As you embark on your journey in affiliate marketing, remember that success is within your reach with dedication, perseverance, and a strategic approach.

**Here are some final words of encouragement to keep you motivated along the way:**

**1. Believe in Yourself:**
- Have confidence in your abilities and believe in your potential to succeed as an affiliate marketer. Trust in your skills, knowledge, and instincts, and don't let self-doubt hold you back.

**2. Embrace the Learning Process:**
- Affiliate marketing is a dynamic and ever-evolving field, so embrace the learning process with curiosity

and enthusiasm. Stay open-minded, continuously educate yourself, and be willing to adapt and evolve as needed.

### 3. Stay Persistent and Resilient:
- Rome wasn't built in a day, and neither is a successful affiliate marketing business. Stay persistent in your efforts, be resilient in the face of challenges, and keep pushing forward even when things get tough.

### 4. Focus on Value and Authenticity:
- Prioritize delivering value to your audience and building authentic relationships based on trust and integrity. Be genuine, transparent, and ethical in your interactions, and always put the needs of your audience first.

### 5. Celebrate Your Wins:
- Celebrate your successes, no matter how small, and acknowledge your progress along the way. Take pride in your achievements, and use them as fuel to propel you forward toward even greater heights.

**6. Surround Yourself with Support:**
- Surround yourself with a supportive network of peers, mentors, and fellow affiliate marketers who can offer guidance, encouragement, and motivation when needed. Collaboration and community are invaluable assets on your journey.

**7. Stay Focused on Your Goals:**
- Keep your goals in sight and stay focused on the bigger picture, even when faced with distractions or setbacks. Visualize your success, set clear objectives, and take consistent action toward achieving your dreams.

**8. Enjoy the Journey:**
- Remember to enjoy the journey and savor the process of building your affiliate marketing business. Celebrate the milestones, learn from the experiences, and find joy in the pursuit of your passions and aspirations.

Affiliate marketing offers a world of opportunities for those willing to seize them. With determination, perseverance, and a positive mindset, you can overcome challenges, achieve your goals, and create the life of your dreams through affiliate marketing. Trust in yourself, stay committed to your vision, and embrace the journey with courage, enthusiasm, and unwavering belief in your ability to succeed. You've got this!

www.ingramcontent.com/pod-product-compliance
Lightning Source LLC
Chambersburg PA
CBHW071207240526
45470CB00018B/1529